'An atlas of creativity that celebrates the best of our wild, unpredictable and generous humanity just at the time that the algorithmic world is trying to tame, predict and cost it.'

Frank Cottrell-Boyce, Screenwriter & Award-Winning Novelist

'A masterclass in harnessing innovation. Essential for leaders aiming to inspire and drive creative excellence.'

Fiona Spooner, Managing Director, Consumer Revenue,
Financial Times

'*A Year of Creativity* is a game changer. Kathryn and Sue have written an important and entertaining book. The best business book I've read this year.'

Rak Patel, Head of Sales, EMEA, Spotify

'Well worth a read for leader looking to unleash creativity and innovation in their organizations. Sue and Kathryn provide a practical guide on how to master the art and science of creativity within business, from their lived experience leading transformations.'

Helen Bentley, Partner, Digital Strategy, Innovation &
Experience Design, EY

'This book ignites innovation, challenging business leaders to embrace creativity as the ultimate competitive advantage. A must-read for forward-thinking executives.'

Larissa Vince, CEO, TBWA London

'A rallying call for creativity in all areas of business, full of useful anecdotes and tips on how everyone can be more creative.'

Phil Hall, UK CEO, Ocean Outdoor

'A book for all seasons – *A Year of Creativity* synthesizes best-in-class thinking designed, no less, to ward off the banishment of wonder! With endless inspiration and provocation packed into its 52 creative techniques, Kathryn and Sue showcase how creativity is a superpower able to drive innovation, and how this intangible force demands positivity and regular flexing. So, if you're ready to ditch the cynicism and lose the ennui, let this book inspire you to step outside your comfort zones and take transformational action.'

Arif Durrani, Global Content Director, Reuters Plus

KATHRYN JACOB AND SUE UNERMAN

A YEAR OF CREATIVITY

52 SMART IDEAS
FOR BOOSTING CREATIVITY, INNOVATION
AND INSPIRATION AT WORK

BLOOMSBURY BUSINESS
LONDON • OXFORD • NEW YORK • NEW DELHI • SYDNEY

BLOOMSBURY BUSINESS
Bloomsbury Publishing Plc
50 Bedford Square, London, WC1B 3DP, UK
29 Earlsfort Terrace, Dublin 2, Ireland

BLOOMSBURY, BLOOMSBURY BUSINESS and the Diana logo are trademarks of
Bloomsbury Publishing Plc

First published in Great Britain 2024

A catalogue record for this book is available from the British Library

Library of Congress Cataloguing-in-Publication data has been applied for

ISBN: HB: 978-1-3994-1325-1; eBook: 978-1-3994-1326-8

2 4 6 8 10 9 7 5 3 1

Typeset by Deanta Global Publishing Services, Chennai, India
Printed and bound in Great Britain by CPI Group (UK) Ltd, Croydon CR0 4YY

To find out more about our authors and books visit www.bloomsbury.com and sign up
for our newsletters

Contents

Foreword

By Josh Goldstine, President of Worldwide Marketing, Warner Bros. Entertainment Inc

Art and Science

We live in a world where we have to balance the two essential tools at our disposal: analytics and creativity.

From advanced machine learning to the latest breakthroughs in generative AI, there is no question that technology is forever changing our world, from how we solve problems to how we drive human behaviour. The insights and possibilities are truly profound and, though perhaps scary at times, nonetheless exciting. Yet for all the promise, technology cannot kill the inherent value of human creativity which empowers us to explore uncharted territory and dream beyond the confines of what has come before. We must always make space for surprise and discovery. Discovery is such an essential and powerful human experience – a bit like falling in love.

In the entertainment business where I work, there is an interesting collision between these two cultures. A collision between Silicon Valley and Hollywood. Netflix sees itself as fundamentally a tech company. Hollywood has been storytelling brilliantly for more than a hundred years. Each of them has more to teach each other than either realize.

Algorithms will tell you what has succeeded in the past and make probabilistic predictions about the future. It is the computer scientist's answer to the philosopher Søren Kierkegaard's observation 'life can only be understood backwards but it must be lived forwards.' But for all the power of algorithms, it is essential that we understand their limits. Because algorithms are inherently backwards-looking they can cause us to miss the new, next thing. No predictive algorithm could have told you that the Beatles would emerge from Liverpool and change the lives of a generation. Or that *E.T.* and *Star Wars* would be the hits that they were to become.

Moreover, recognizing a pattern is quite different from understanding *why* the pattern occurred in the first place. Following a recipe does not make you a chef. Understanding the ingredients, their properties and appeal, allows one to create novel mixtures that truly surprise and delight. Creativity plays an essential role.

I went to Harvard to be a scientist, mostly to satisfy a vision of me that my father had. I quickly realized that while I have an analytical side of my brain, I wanted to study the things that I truly loved: film, storytelling, philosophy.

I entered the movie business and found myself in marketing. I began my career making movie trailers and what I learned is that you can position a movie so many different ways – make so many different creative executions of trailers for the same movie. By combining this process of creative ideation with market research, statistical analysis and machine learning, it would become clear which story elements generated the necessary emotional engagement and broadest audience appeal to maximize ticket sales and box office results. Effectively, mixing *art* and *science* was the key ingredient to my early success.

As patterns emerged, I became incredibly curious about which stories connected with a mass audience and, most importantly, *why*. I discovered interesting parallels between what Claude Lévi-Strauss, the father of structural anthropology, had to say about the concept of myth and my own observations about what worked in movie marketing: relatable real-life problems and the promise of some imaginary resolution. We gravitate to stories that seek to transcend the limitations of our ordinary existence, the intractable problems of everyday life. This is the so-called 'escapism' that Hollywood delivers. Tech may reveal the patterns, but we need Art to explore the wish fulfilment that drives our hopes and dreams.

The other challenge I have experienced with a purely analytic approach is that it focuses so heavily on efficiency, and who is most likely to be interested, that it runs the risk of preaching to the choir and failing to maximize the potential audience. Even the most sophisticated algorithms cannot replace the work of truly creative and breakthrough marketing, whose job is to drive conversion and create new audiences. As the advertising guru George Lois put it: 'Great advertising can make food taste better, can make your car run smoother. It can change your perception of something.'

There is a space between what might be predicted through analytics and what can possibly be achieved. What Art has to teach Tech is not how to most *efficiently* get the people most likely to engage, but rather how to *effectively* change the minds of the least likely but still attainable. *Data makes you a thermometer; creativity makes you a thermostat.*

Nowhere was this more apparent to me than our recent success with the *Barbie* marketing campaign. If you had asked audiences what they expected of a movie about the iconic toy, they would have said something for children, or a movie that was akin to the Barbie cartoons, or they would tell you their disapproval of how Barbie was said to objectify women's bodies. The movie's audience would have been inherently narrow, and *Barbie* would have been a flop.

But the creators Greta Gerwig, Noah Baumbach and Margot Robbie had much bigger ambitions for the movie. Greta used the IP of the iconic plastic doll to tell a much larger and more compelling story about the state of being a woman. She made a profound and empowering comedy that promoted the idea that we are 'enough' simply by being human and that our individuality is to be celebrated.

The question for the marketing campaign was clear: how do we break through the perceived notions of the movie?

We had to create the space for novelty and to say something truly different. If we had just done what was expected, we would never have spoken to the breadth of audiences that we did or created the worldwide sensation.

To pierce the zeitgeist, we had to kick off the campaign with something bold and unexpected. We are a herd species – sometimes the herd rumbles, but if you achieve a tipping point, extraordinary and unpredictably massive movement can happen.

We ran a teaser trailer in the most unexpected place – the 2022 *Avatar* movie, an epic sci-fi adventure driven largely by males, where you would least imagine a conventional *Barbie Movie* to show up. But this wasn't a conventional *Barbie Movie*. The trailer was highly controversial among many of my colleagues: a *2001* parody, bold, dissonant and unexpected. Every single territory around the world urged me not to do it.

But it defied people's expectations – it spoke to relatable human truths but unlike anything you'd ever seen before. It was not the trailer for *Barbie* that anyone expected. No predictive algorithm could ever have come up with this idea.

We branded the movie around pink, and the swell of pink around the world was quite extraordinary. We created a cultural permission slip through numerous memes, cultural engagement and third-party tie-ins from Progressive Insurance to Google.

Movies are incredibly expensive to make. The fate of the movie rests on the opening weekend. If audiences don't show up (like an election) on opening day we lose. Success cannot just be about how efficient we can be but how big a success can we make this. For *Barbie* we set an audacious goal to be the biggest female-driven movie ever, and we shattered all records.

Truth is, I have doubts every day, but that anxiety is part of what drives excellence. You're not achieving anything if the bar is too low. If the bar is at a reasonable level, what fun is that? Being human is going faster, being better.

I'm very much against the idea of analytics versus creativity. The challenge of the moment is how you combine them in the best ways. People say that every movie is as different as every snowflake, but also there are patterns of snowflakes. We do lots of analysis, but everything is always changing. There are rules and exceptions to the rules. The question is how do you understand the deeper truth of the rule? (The Delphic oracle was always right, you just had to interpret her meaning.)

There is not one objective reality that data can predict, but of course it is very useful to make things a little less random. It is all about finding the balance between Art and Science. The insights of data and Silicon Valley combined with Hollywood and Barnum & Bailey emotional engagement gives you an edge.

I love what I do, everything changes, and everything evolves.

Kathryn and Sue's book is all about the necessities of integrating creative practices into your organization in order to take things to the next level. We need to be open to this, and to be ambitious and brave about change to lift what we do from efficient and safe to excellent and innovative. This book is full of practical ways to drive creative brilliance in your workplace, to break through convention to lift your work to something really exceptional. And injecting creativity into your workplace will ensure that you love what you do.

Introduction

This is why *A Year of Creativity* is worth your time.

Most businesses have leadership teams skilled in analytics and logic. It makes sense. The language of the board room in big businesses requires this, and even in small organizations the majority of people at the top lean towards traditional left-brain or analytical skills – the skills that are measured by success in examinations and traditional teaching methods. This is fine, but it lacks balance. Too much left-brain analytical thinking means that right-brain thinking, gut instinct and the kind of creativity that can lead to step changes are less valued. If every decision is based on evidence and proven techniques, there isn't any room for judgements based on instinct guided by experience which can lead to real improvements and new ways of moving forward. This book will give you the opportunity to stop looking in the rear-view mirror only, and instead create exponential growth and innovation.

We are living through a rapidly changing era where artificial intelligence (AI) and large learning models (LLM) like ChatGPT and Bard, among others, are revolutionizing working practices. However, when everyone is using these tools, where is the edge that can lift your business above the norm? The answer lies in developing your own creativity, and that of your team. It's you who can make the difference.

People sometimes misunderstand creativity. This book explains that all creativity comes from somewhere, and often from mashing up different existing ideas from different places, to create something new. Every creative person stands on the shoulders of others. This is how creativity and innovation works, it is to be encouraged. We are grateful for every creative person who has helped make this book what it is.

Nearly everyone we have encountered has contributed to this book in some way. Especially we have been inspired by Brian Eno and Peter Schmidt's Oblique Strategies (*see* p.176).

Perhaps the overriding reason to adopt the strategies of this book is that it will make you happier. You unlock a part of yourself that isn't bound by rules or custom, that is open to possibility. It's more fun to work with creativity, and your team will benefit from this as well. Therefore, of course, so will your clients, customers, suppliers and partners.

Creativity is easier than you think. There are many myths and rituals around creativity, some of which are merely there to discourage and keep the circle of creative thinkers exclusive. Don't be unconfident or discouraged. This book will give you the techniques you need to be as creative as anyone.

There are no gatekeepers to creativity any more. A decade ago there were many barriers to creativity. A few glossy magazine editors or designers were the arbiters of choice for the world. In the last few years, however, there has been an explosion in all kinds of content on the internet and social media. Now the single most popular form of content worldwide is user-generated – that is, videos, blogs, podcasts, images, songs, dances, art, all made by people like you.

You are a creative talent. You might not think so, but you are. All it takes is getting yourself and your teams ready for creativity – and we will show you how, and then how to practise going out of your comfort zone gently by following the techniques in the book. Most adults don't discover a new talent in life once they are grown up and in the workplace. Especially if they have ever been told: *No, you aren't the creative one.* This is your opportunity to experience the unlocking of your potential. Or to exercise it further, and in more meaningful ways. To see the results of your new approach and for you and your colleagues to be different and distinguishable. To have an edge.

Get ready for creativity. Your authors are experienced business-women, iconic in their own sectors, who have published bestselling books on workplace culture. They are big proponents of accountability, data analysis and empiricism. They also encourage creativity, going outside the normal rules of the sector, and have delivered award-winning campaigns. Creativity matters. It has been underemphasized in many businesses and workplaces, and practising it will go beyond the normal limits of the day job to drive advantage, enjoyment and innovation. The techniques in this book are pragmatic, proven and simple to follow.

PART ONE

CHAPTER ONE

The case for creativity in business

Creativity in business. Not a fad, not an adjunct. Vital, crucial, necessary.

Fans of the football club Barcelona may recall a game in 2012 when their team played Chelsea in the semi-final of the European Champions League. It's probably fair to say that most people who watched the game, excluding Chelsea fans, were rooting for Barcelona, a team that was then playing some of the most beautiful football in the world.

Sue watched her partner watch the game. At the end of it, he was yelling, 'Just stick it in the mixer!' She had to ask him what that meant. He said that the Barcelona players were known for their passing game and keeping possession of the ball. The players knew what worked, and what didn't, and played to a system that made them extraordinarily successful. Unfortunately for Barcelona, the only team that understood Barcelona's system better than Barcelona was Chelsea.

Their fans were desperate for Barcelona to change tack and take some chances – to stick it in the mixer (goal area) and not worry about giving the ball away. But it wasn't to be; the best team does not always win.

Their failure offers an object lesson.

Beyond the football pitch and across the globe, how many glaring opportunities are passing us by because established systems or playbooks mean that people are reluctant to try something new or untested, to 'stick it in the mixer'?

If you want to win at work – and beyond – this year and the next, efficiency is not enough, strategy is not enough, analysis is not enough. We live in times of complexity and ambiguity. Even those businesses that have themselves been major disruptors fear major new disruption themselves. No bets are certain. In response, leaders are battening down the hatches. Incremental change seems safer: the more uncertain the world, the more they retreat to the principles of analysis and the need for detailed proof of any concept.

This is a big mistake. This is not the time to have faith in heritage practices. This is not a time to make assumptions based on the experiences of the past. Safety is an illusion, and nothing is guaranteed. Just ask that Barcelona team.

There is an alternative.

The only way to secure competitive advantage is to ensure that **creative thinking** is driving your business. Sometimes you need to break with analysis and just 'stick it in the mixer'.

Into the unknown

A Year of Creativity argues that following the rules and justifying actions on the basis of known data will take you only so far; everyone needs to learn when and how to take a leap of faith into the unknown. And to understand that this creativity is not enough when it is just deployed for a five-year plan, or an annual away day.

Creativity needs to be baked into everything we do all year round, whether we're problem-solving, looking for inspiration at work or navigating personal or family difficulties. Sometimes, most of the time, sticking to the tried and true is good and proper. Yet this is based on what we know we already know; it's much less useful when you're faced with uncertainty.

Instead, as we might conclude from the beautiful game, sometimes you need to stick it in the mixer for any chance of a win. Know what you are doing, but also be clear about what you don't know and when to try something where you cannot predict the outcome.

Unexpected disruption is now a fact of life. Shopping for goods and services, for example, has changed, and is changing. By 2025 three billion people will be shopping online. And that space is becoming more crowded, and more competitive. People spend more time with media channels than they used to, but there is a limit to the hours in the day and their levels of attention are much lower and variable than 20 years ago.

And the rules of many sectors are revolutionizing. Pop star Kate Bush enjoyed renewed success for her song 'Running Up That Hill' because it featured in Netflix's *Stranger Things*. When the song was first released in 1985, radio play and reviews drove sales; now it's just as likely to be Netflix and Spotify. Most of our brands and markets are vulnerable. Google research concludes that 81 per cent of brands could disappear tomorrow and no one would care. And this is true across every sector.

To tackle this uncertain world, we all need to get serious about creativity.

Towards creative leadership

Two kinds of leadership are fundamental to organizations. This second form of leadership is crucial, but often overlooked. This is predominantly for one of two reasons.

First, creativity is often perceived to be the responsibility of an elite team, protected from the rigour of business and charged with delivering some 'magic'. This team will itself shut down creative suggestions from outside the clique, and at the same time continually complain that their ideas are destroyed by demands for accountability from spreadsheet analysts. (As we will show, creativity and accountability are entirely compatible.)

Second, there may be creative thinking throughout the organization but ideas fail at the final hurdle because of loss aversion (a bias that makes us feel loss more acutely than gain) and a lack of risk appetite.

Left-brain thinking, which loves order, likes to shut down right-brain creativity. Left-brain thinkers tend to swamp right-brain thinkers with logic and proof points, because you can't prove something new until you try it out.

At the same time, and perhaps understandably in the current economic climate, most people at work do not consider themselves to be creative. Adobe Research shows a global creativity crisis: 8 in 10 people feel that unlocking creativity is critical to economic growth and nearly two-thirds of respondents feel creativity is valuable to society. Yet a striking minority – only 1 in 4 people – believe they are living up to their own creative potential.

A key message of *A Year of Creativity* is that **everyone** is creative.

Don't believe us? If you ever ask a bunch of kindergarten kids about art and creativity, the chances are that they'll all stick their hands up. By the time they reach early teens, however, most kids don't call themselves creative, and those that do are worried about what their peers think of them. Everyone has creative instincts – yet, like any muscle, if these are not used, they will atrophy.

Most people aren't asked to use their creativity at work. At the start of your career, you're normally required to carry out specific instructions, and veering from them is frowned upon, even possibly raising a black mark on career progression. If you're rewarded for doing as you are told, then that's the behaviour you will continue to deliver.

Yet in these highly challenging times everyone needs to think creatively. The challenges and opportunities of tomorrow are not answered by heritage behaviour.

Nor can we simply rely on a new era of data maturity to provide the answers for us. Artificial intelligence (AI) certainly allows much decision-making to be automated, at speed and at scale. Take a trip abroad, for example. In the 1950s you would have to visit your bank and change money into travellers' cheques. In the 1990s you could use your credit card abroad, but if you had not informed your bank that you were travelling in the first place your credit card would be frozen.

Today, thanks to fintech innovation and artificial intelligence, your bank cards will work seamlessly in most cases everywhere in the world.

But as better AI fuels more of the workplace, a paradox arises. *The Paradox of Automation* recognizes that automation can be a positive, with fewer people needed for mundane jobs that robots can carry out faster and tirelessly. But when something goes wrong, we're more reliant than ever on human judgement and creativity to spot mistakes, correct them and improve systems for the future.

Efficient automation makes humans more important, not less. It also levels the playing field in mature markets, meaning that competitive advantage lies in those organizations which fuel differentiation with creativity.

How then do you harness creativity, not for the sake of it, but to drive value and growth for your organization and your own career? *A Year of Creativity* will get your creative muscles active, and keep them fit and useful all year round.

Creativity is seen as fluffy or elite – both those views are wrong

The view of creativity as 'fluffy' can feel prevalent. There are many theories as to why that way of thinking exists. One is that many people used to work in roles largely driven by routine or process, meaning that those activities considered decorative or which did not produce something practical were not valued. Who needs a new painting or book when there are so many of them already? (Perhaps unsurprisingly, your authors have very strong views on the need for new books.) People who want a pragmatic and process-oriented output from society will ask: 'What use can we make of that?'. Of course, there is a process in creativity too. If you read about the output of certain artists, they used teams around them to deliver the works of art that they were commissioned to deliver. This is why you come across artworks that have been attributed to well-known artists but which are found to have been painted largely by pupils of theirs, who are taking the style and manner of their art and delivering a version of it. There were artist assistants in the heyday of portrait painting who specialized in painting fabric, backgrounds and pets. This is clearly a process rather than a case of unprompted brilliance that was delivered to the canvas.

As we'll discuss in another part of the book, there are elements of creativity that can't be measured. This contributes to the notion that it is fluffy. Our ways of working are becoming more data-focused now that computing has made possible the assimilation of large amounts of data. Creativity doesn't fit well with a data-driven outlook. How do you measure the impact a new idea can have before it's put into action? Ideas can feel, and seem, ephemeral – and from their abstraction the perception of fluffiness can emerge.

Elitism is also a charge levelled about creativity. As a small number of people can, for example, paint or write music – of the types that people want to look at or listen to, at least – that gift of creativity can feel excluding and distinctly 'other' to most people. Another contributory factor is that in the past a career of creativity wasn't open to most people; they needed to earn regular salaries to support themselves. Vincent Van Gogh sold a handful of paintings in his lifetime and died in poverty. The reality is that for most people, even those with the ability to be creative, the option wasn't viable. So, creativity came to be seen as a rare quality, akin to a mythical quality or way of being. On the other hand, creativity was also considered a possibility only for those not living a normal life, with the expectations that brought. The usual perception was that a life of creativity is one apart from regular people. That situation does not reflect today's reality, though – all of us now have the tools to spread our ideas just by using our mobile phones. In fact, the most popular form of content today is created by people like you and me, not by professionals. There are still people who are capable of creating better cat videos than most of us, and they are the ones who get the most likes.

Our working world is one where it can feel safer to make incremental changes, waiting for a competitor to change before taking that risk ourselves (and then hoping that we can make a change too, in the hope of catching up). In that working scenario, creativity has no perceived value. Yet in a study done by Singer and McCallum for Deloitte, respondents with high growth (defined as having annual revenue growth of +10 per cent or more) are much more likely to have creativity embedded, in contrast to their negative growth peers. They view creative ideas as essential for driving long-term growth and are more likely to have encouraged cross-functional collaboration. They also have a higher level of willingness to embrace risk.

For an example of creativity in action, the story of Stagekings is relevant. In March 2020, the Australian Prime Minister, faced with the COVID epidemic, placed a ban on gatherings of more than 500 people. For Stagekings (the name is a clue), this meant a loss of their main operation overnight – building stage sets for most of the biggest events in Australia. Seeing that the epidemic was now making more people work from home, Stagekings pivoted, and started to make flat-packed assemble-it-yourself furniture to meet the demands of running a home office, answering the needs of a market that hadn't been in existence just months before. This new venture, IsoKing, grew so quickly that they needed more employees and in the first year of operation, the company generated revenues of AU$3.6 million, a higher figure than the original company had generated. More people employed, more money made – that was the value of this piece of creative thinking.

More than that, a creative approach can help bring a company together behind a shared vision. If you knew you were making a brand-new and highly innovative car which would change the experience of driving, that is far more compelling than making a couple of minor changes to the dashboard and introducing a new colour option for the seats. It might look like change but it won't make you leap out of bed, excited for the future. Nor will consumers look at each other and demand to be taken to the showroom immediately.

We need to see creativity as a way of approaching points of transition in our companies. That transition may be a change to our way of working, or a way of discovering new markets. It's not just for the elite . . . or the fluffy.

Creativity doesn't mean immediate returns – is it even measurable?

We live in a world where measurement is present in everything we do. How many steps we take, how far we walk and even what type of sleep we had last night. You can measure anything and everything, all the time. This means that the return we want on ideas and the intangible nature of creativity are in conflict. If I can tell you how much time I spent on my computer last week, why can't I estimate the return of three brainstorms? Is there a measure of return which I can use to grade our ideas and idea creation? Also, when do all these sessions pay off?

We have bad news on this, we're afraid. Unlike your sleep counter, there isn't a grading available on the type of idea that you can create or that you decide to implement. You need to be conscious of where you start from and where you could end up. If your company or division has never undertaken any type of creativity exercise before, how are you to be judged against another company where creativity is part of their daily output? You aren't in the same space as them – and you need to be conscious of that and to decide where your aspirations lie.

There are psychological tests that are said to be able to determine if a person is creative. These involve exploring how original, flexible and detailed their thinking is by asking an unusual question; for example, think of how many uses there are for a milk carton (apart from storing milk, obviously). These resources can explore your capabilities as an individual, but they can't judge your creative output. Finding a new packaging concept is different in its demands to changing your electric car design. Yet both are creative ideas even though they have different measures of whether there is a return. In the case of the new car design, this creative process and its product will take years to reach the market. There will be no immediate return. Also, their measure of return will be different and will need contextualizing in the wider market where they operate. Creativity for the sake of creativity may have no immediate value; however, not having any framing around your expectations is equally foolish. Creativity is a weapon, but it can't perform magic on its own.

It can be useful to map your expectations around creativity and how it connects with all the other aspects of your operations. In deciding to be more creative, your company needs to think about the pillars of *people*, *product* and *process*. If you're expecting creative returns without those elements in line with your expectations, then your measurement process will be even harder. However, making creativity more prevalent might have an unexpected return in terms of your team members. All steps towards more forward-thinking and dynamic operations can have an impact on your colleagues. Ask anyone who has ever worked in a place where *If it ain't broke, don't fix it (or improve it, or keep up with market changes)* is the mantra – they will tell you how soul-destroying and unmotivating that thought process is. Small steps, which may not count as a *return*, can be a whole new direction. For your people, your products, and your processes.

One method of mapping measurement is to see if creativity as a tool will deliver your goals. If you're trying to measure whether creativity can drive up your share price to a certain level within six months, is that even possible? Any number of factors can affect that metric and even the most effective creativity can't address a political challenge to your sector, such as restrictions on your product range. You can use creativity to change that product, but to do that in six months is probably too big an ask of your teams and processes.

Go through your business plans and be realistic and logical – two adjectives not normally associated with the creative process – about what role enhancing your creativity can play. Draw up a timeline, but do not be too optimistic about it. Realism is your friend in these situations. Is creativity going to deliver a marginal improvement in six months, building momentum over the long term? Perhaps. The seminal Apple '1984' advertising campaign was based on visions about that iconic year, made famous by the George Orwell novel. It had immediate impact, and over the years has been cited as one of the definitive moments in Apple's history, setting a tone and creating a feeling around the company and its values that still resonates today. How many other things have we seen from 40 years ago that are part of a value system and market definition? That people still remember and talk about? Did the creativity resonate at the time? Yes, absolutely. Does it still resonate today? Yes, it does.

In another field, Coco Chanel put women into casual, comfortable clothing that was quick and easy to put on (and take off). She changed the way that women saw themselves – even today, when women ask about feeling good, the advice is always to wear something that you feel comfortable in and which allows you to move freely. A line could be drawn from the designs of Chanel in the 1920s to the athleisure way of dressing that is so familiar today. Creativity can have many iterations, some of them a long way from the original intention.

When we are approaching creativity, we need to establish the place that we come from as the base of our measurement. Are we coming from a creative-free zone or seeking to build creativity? Those different starting points will change the gradation of our measurements, as well as the goals that creativity can help us achieve. There may be intangibles that creativity helps – a sense of being part of a team, an individual's sense of growing confidence when they see their capabilities growing. Those things might not be a return in terms of the sense usual, but they do have a value.

Marginal gains, or the Fosbury flop

We have observed two kinds of change in the workplace. The most common, and perhaps the most easily adopted, is the principle of marginal gains.

There are some famous sporting proponents of this.

Sir David Brailsford is the former performance director of the British cycling team during its multiple award-winning years between 2003 and 2014. He is famous for using data to drive performance. His philosophy is to break down every component of an athlete's environment and behaviour, and seek to improve each element by 1 per cent. This included providing pillows for the cyclists to sleep on when they travelled, removing dust from every environment, monitoring the moods and emotions of every team member. Brailsford says: 'The whole principle came from the idea that if you broke down everything you could think of that goes into riding a bike, and then improved it by 1 per cent, you will get a significant increase when you put them all together.'

His team won two cycling gold medals in 2004, their best performance in nearly a century. Under his leadership the cycling team continued to improve, winning multiple world championships and leading the medal table at the 2008 and 2012 Olympics. Its popularity led to an increase in everyday cycling too, something that Brailsford says is one of his proudest achievements.

And he's not the only proponent of incremental gains and studying statistics to look for untapped improvements. Sir Clive Woodward was the coach of the England Rugby team between 1997 and 2004, managing the team's World Cup victory in 2003. He delivered a transformation in terms of professionalism, including mandating that team members turned up early for meetings, that players who weren't picked for the team congratulated their rivals who were, and keeping their language clean. He also looked for *critical non-essentials*, where there were opportunities for marginal gains. For example, he commissioned skintight kit, making it more difficult for players to be tackled than when they were wearing baggy shirts. And he made the team change kit for the second half so that they went back onto the pitch with a fresh state of mind. Woodward said: 'Winning the Rugby world cup was not about doing one thing 100 per cent better, but about doing 100 things 1 per cent better.'

The philosophy behind *MoneyBall: The Art of Winning an Unfair Game*, by Michael Lewis, also focuses on looking at the details of data for improvements. Published in 2003, it describes the huge successes that Oakland Athletics baseball team achieved under general manager Billy Beane. The focus is on sabermetrics – detailed empirical analysis of statistics to find ways to beat the competition. However, the very success of this technique, and of course of other marginal gains from statistics, leads to its downfall too. The more famous these techniques become, the more likely your competitors are to adopt them too.

Initially, baseball was transformed by this technique. In fact, in 2002, the Oakland Athletics, who had a salary bill of $44 million, were competitive with much larger teams who spent over $125 million on players. But when your analytical techniques become successful, they become susceptible to copying.

Author and journalist Derek Thompson says *Moneyball* has ruined baseball for him. And also the music charts; he's an expert here with his book *Hit Makers: The Science of Popularity in an Age of Distraction*. In fact, in his opinion, it has ruined most forms of entertainment, and pretty much culture in general.

The book and the 2011 film inspired the same precision of insight into a wealth of other areas to create significant competitive advantage. Once everyone is practising precision data analysis, there is no longer significant breakthrough advantage. It just becomes table stakes.

Thompson argues that the 'analytics revolution, which began with the movement known as Moneyball, led to a series of offensive and defensive adjustments that were, let's say, *catastrophically successful*' – and took the unpredictability and pizzazz from the game of baseball.

Once everyone is looking at the same data, more easily achieved with large learning models (LLM) and AI, then everyone can access the same marginal gains.

So, incremental improvements are good, and necessary, but they are not enough.

To stick with sport, sometimes you need a Fosbury flop: a complete revolution, a literally backward flip that breaks all the conventional ways in which the category behaves.

The Fosbury flop is a jumping style in high jump. Until 1968 all the athletes competed in this event using the straddle technique or scissors jump. In 1968, at the Mexico Olympics, Dick Fosbury introduced a new technique, jumping backwards off the 'wrong' foot and arching his body over the bar, face up. Fosbury had been practising the technique for a number of years, partly because he wasn't a naturally talented high jumper. In fact, he'd failed to make it onto his local athletic club's high school jump team as a schoolboy. His new technique allowed him to use the natural arch of his back to propel himself higher. Fosbury won gold and set a new world record of 2.24 metres (or 7ft 4¼ inches). His technique had ripped up decades of high jump orthodoxy.

This is an important process to bear in mind when you are surrounded by orthodoxy. Whenever you come across practices that are justified by *Well, that is the way we have always done things*, Fosbury should inspire you to ask why, and then why again. The default scenarios won't lead to exponential advantage. Challenge convention and introduce creativity. When everyone has the same data, your twist on interpreting the results can lead to significant advantage.

The problem with brainstorming

Perhaps the most famous technique for idea generation, and the most mocked in TV shows such as *The Office* is the brainstorm. Lots of organizations use this exercise in some form to come up with new ideas, but it isn't a panacea – in fact it might be the very opposite – and so we want to deal with it now. It's a traditional and much used method for creativity. A group of people meet up and use flip charts, Post-it notes and Sharpies to come up with creative ideas.

Search online for how to brainstorm, and 68 million answers come up. Amazon.com lists over 500 books of techniques. There are many 'rules of the game', and probably a dozen brainstorms going on somewhere near your place of work right now.

A group activity, the brainstorm is a session of up to a dozen people where everyone is encouraged to come up with spontaneous ideas to solve a problem or deliver change. The idea is not to think any of your ideas through, but to blurt them out. The moderator of the brainstorm has a duty to capture every idea and give encouragement and endorsement by writing them up.

We have been involved in many brainstorming sessions. We have led and conducted many brainstorms. The truth is that it's a good way of giving people a shared sense of problem-solving. It's also a relatively pleasant way of passing a few hours at work. Usually, it encourages enthusiasm and involvement. There's just one problem: it really isn't that great a way of coming up with creative ideas.

One reason is this: *No idea is a bad idea* is one of the sacred rules of brainstorming.

The concept is based on the theory that ideas are like young plants. Rain too hard on them, and they will wilt away. Don't criticize. Warm them in the greenhouse of sunshine approval. This is one of the founding rules laid down for brainstorms by Alex Osborn of ad agency BBDO, who coined the term in 1948 – and it is still widely employed today (together with the other rules which are to emphasize quantity of ideas, to allow freewheeling thinking and to build on the ideas of others). While other techniques for the sessions will vary, these rules usually prevail.

This is despite a relatively little-known study conducted as long ago as 2000 which seems to prove the opposite of what we tend to believe, or at least are told as one of the principle rules of brainstorming. Criticism does not deter ideas. In fact, it encourages them. In an academic experiment 'The liberating role of conflict in group creativity' by Charlan Nemeth, individuals in small groups were given the problem of solving traffic congestion. The research was conducted in San Francisco and Paris. The rules were the same except for a test set of groups who were told to feel free to debate and even to criticize each other's ideas.

Most creativity coaches and moderators would predict that allowing criticism and challenges would be the death of ideas. In fact, in these carefully controlled conditions, the reverse was true. Allowing debate led to more ideas, significantly more. These results may seem surprising. However, given these two requirements for creativity, they are no surprise.

The first requirement is diversity of thinking. The second is authenticity, to be yourself.

If people in the brainstorm are similar in how they think rather than diverse, this may well make for an easier, and perhaps happier, session, but there will be fewer different ideas.

Furthermore, if the people in the brainstorm are not similar in how they think, *but* have been asked to follow a rule that they must not debate or criticize, then they may well be self-censoring to ensure a happy and obedient session. The effort required in worrying about not offending others by a spontaneous negative reaction to ideas can suppress creativity. This doesn't mean criticism is required, just that people don't have to stop themselves being critical. The *Don't rain on ideas* rule can be replaced by a *Don't take criticism personally* mandate. Everyone should be free to be themselves and to say what they really think, with courtesy and kindness, but also with the courage of their convictions.

Think hard before your next idea generation session. Is the required outcome and priority that people should have a good time? If so, definitely keep to the standard rules. But if you have a real need for creativity and a diverse range of solutions, then it's definitely worth breaking the *No idea is a bad idea* rule.

The author of the study says that she believes that disagreements open the mind: 'Faced with an alternative conception of reality and a different way of thinking . . . we actually search for and consider more options.'

Extroverts tend to thrive better in brainstorms than introverts. Interrupters tend to get more ideas out than non-interrupters. If you like to live spontaneously, you'll enjoy them more than careful planners. All of this limits the range of ideas that will be produced.

Sheena Iyengar, a professor at Columbia Business School, has compiled academic research on idea generation, including a decade of interviews with more than a thousand people. She concludes that group brainstorming is usually a waste of time. She points out that the ethos of brainstorming – suck up any judgement and build on what others say – is better suited to 'polite conversation at a dinner party' than to problem-solving at work. She says: 'You do not get your best ideas out of freewheeling brainstorming sessions.'

Enthusiasm is brilliant at work, and creativity belongs to everyone. But within the constraints of a brainstorm the tension of coming up with original ideas that please the boss can be enormous and makes the chances of creative thought even harder than usual. In *W1A*, the wonderful spoof TV show about the BBC, a team of PR specialists are made to play a game of ping-pong with the twist that they have to come up with a new idea for a show every time they hit the ball. The US series of *The Office* spoofed idea generation too with a ludicrous episode where the team have to come up with an 'urgent' idea for the boss, Michael, to write in wet cement before the cement dries.

Brainstorms can have a role to play, they do make people feel involved, and they can be fun. But they aren't going to get you new ideas.

Elite creative teams are not the answer either

Another tradition of creativity that needs to be dismantled is the idea of elite creative teams. Often these are designed for best intentions, to create a kind of talent moat whereby those blessed with strong creativity can be protected from the outside world.

There are three things wrong with this from the start. First the idea that one person is creative and others are not. As you'll see throughout this book, we are convinced that everyone can and indeed should be thought of as creative. Second problem with this is that you can't actually protect so-called creative ideas from reality. If they can't exist in the organization's culture, then they will never progress from *nice idea* to *real change*. And finally, there is no such thing as a talent moat in a thriving culture. Because just as a bad culture is infectious and can make everyone miserable, a great culture is blissfully infectious too. If the workplace is driven by creativity, then everyone benefits. It shouldn't be in a separate department, or even on a separate floor; it needs to be *everyone's* job. Because, as we will see later, it makes everyone's job more fun and more rewarding.

Back in the mid-1980s, a large advertising agency was taken over by another company. A big away day was arranged and everyone was invited. Frankie Howerd, the UK TV personality and comedian, was hired to make everyone laugh. The joint chief executives gave a speech, and said that the whole point of the ad agency was to make brilliant, award-winning adverts. Everything and everyone needed to serve this aim. But the department responsible for these ideas was a small subsection of the whole agency. It's hard to see how anyone outside that elite team would have had any idea how to contribute to this worthy aim. As the day wore on, and more speeches were given, some people lost focus and concentration. If creativity was about a group of people in which most staff members were not included, what had it got to do with them? In those days, most creative departments were staffed mainly by men. This has changed somewhat, but not nearly enough. And the problem with this was – and to an extent still is – that this exclusiveness not only excludes but also makes it difficult to generate really creative ideas. How can ideas be creative if everyone in the team looks and sounds the same?

We are big believers in diversity and inclusion. Not only because it is the right thing to do, but also because people from different backgrounds, with different ideas and assumptions, do generate more creative ideas than you get from a homogenous team.

You also need creative thinking to be open to challenge. And challenge can be difficult. As strategist Mark Earls points out, human beings love to copy each other. It's natural. In his book *Copy, Copy, Copy* he gives many examples, including explaining that copying is one of our species' 'greatest gifts and one of the factors most responsible for our success'. Professor Andrew Meltzoff demonstrated that babies as young as 42 minutes old will copy facial gestures like sticking their tongue out and opening their mouths wide.

So, copying helps us learn, and makes us feel safe, part of a tribe. It's also much easier. Deciding for yourself, and calculating probabilities about what the outcome of new actions will be, takes significant mental processing. That's why we spend lots of time either doing what we have done before (copying your past self – if you always have the same pasta at your favourite Italian restaurant, you're defaulting to what you know rather than taking a risk on the new) or doing what everyone else is doing (*How can everyone else be wrong?*).

Sticking to existing heuristics, or rules of thumb, limits us. And having a team that is all alike might be great for banter or feeling like there is a gang of you at work, but it's limiting for creativity.

Every time we jump to consensus, we can miss opportunities for driving the ideas forward. Matthew Syed clarifies this in *Rebel Ideas: the power of diverse thinking*. If we surround ourselves only with those who think like us, life is an echo chamber – and that gets you literally nowhere in terms of getting to grips with the grim realities of today's chaotic times.

The ancient Jewish court the Sanhedrin had diversity of thinking baked in. If there was a unanimous vote to convict the accused, the verdict was thrown out and the accused was exonerated, walking away free. The assumption was that if no one could speak in favour of the accused, the jury had developed group thinking. Group thinking is, of course, unfair and unhelpful. Yet we love to agree with each other. It's a basic human instinct; a remnant perhaps of the necessities for survival of the tribe in Stone Age times.

Every time a team ends up agreeing too fast, the opportunity for a new unthought-of route is lost. Every time you vote on ideas in a workshop openly, and everyone can see which ideas have the most votes, the chance of real innovation is diminished. Innovation and herd behaviour don't mix. If no one can find an issue with the consensus solution, maybe you haven't looked hard enough. If you only ever hear from your team that they agree with you, you're surely not getting the best out of them.

Design for disagreement is a crucial stage for building new ideas. If there is too much focus on consensus the lost opportunity might cost you the future.

Too much agreement, and a lack of interaction with the real world, doesn't help creativity. Just because things have been done this way in the past, is no reason to continue to work this way. In the nineteenth century the leading artists of the day (men) questioned whether it was possible for women to be artists. In fact, women weren't allowed to attend life drawing classes until the twentieth century. This didn't stop them being creative, though, or stop creativity in other fields outside of painting.

If there is a set way of delivering creativity in your organization, it might be time to break it up and experiment with change.

Meaningless creativity

This is a challenging topic for a book talking about how important creativity is, but stick with us. One factor for the cynical or dismissive view of creativity is the way that it is positioned to us as an audience. Creativity is seen as 'different' and not available to most people. Some of this is no doubt due to long held perceptions around the nature and source of the creative process – Plato wrote that Socrates got his creativity from divine inspiration. The Muses breathed creativity into him and gave him the tools that he used to create his works. As Muses aren't readily available as source material in most workplaces, what chance do the rest of us have? We must leave it to the gifted, the ones chosen by the gods, it seems.

This perception also creates one of the problems with creative thinking. It is assumed that any creative thought – particularly one that appears to come from nowhere – has validity. A quick survey of some dubious ideas of recent times, demonstrates the assumption that *new* must be better than what we currently have. This can be a key factor in failure, as the desire for something different may blind us to the reality of how that idea will unfold in our day-to-day lives. The balance between *stay in your lane* and the jump to a random idea appears to be difficult to judge. You want change, so you do something that no one expected. Without the balance of experience and insight, though, it's easy to get lost in the creative experience. One of the last century's most renowned creative talents, Schopenhauer, pointed out that artists must have technical skills, first and foremost, before allowing themselves to give themselves up to creativity – there must be an equity between those two points. As Schopenhauer is hardly known for making his work an easy step from everyday listening, he represents a sustained push to embrace the new and different.

Perhaps the frustration of this concept comes from a blurring between novelty and creativity. How many times have we seen a product or idea labelled as *new*, the improvement implied being *new* as the main differentiation? *New* might not be better, in fact. *New* could just be a bigger range of colour choices on a product that might be unreliable. It's hard to accept that novelty might not have any worth, as people feel that an ever-expanding choice range is a sign of more personalization and options; that a product is trying to be more relevant to us, to make our experiences better. For some consumers, a redesigned home page on a website is not as important as having a booking system that works and which helps you achieve your aims quickly.

Meaningless creativity comes from a sense that any change is good change. It's the perception that doing something new – anything new, really – will change your current trajectory. The foundation of meaningless creativity is a confusion of thought. From that point it's a simple step to generate a myriad of outcomes that give creativity a bad reputation.

We need to find the language and behaviours to challenge meaningless creativity. It can be hard, in the middle of a session on *What's next?* or *Future Directions*, to articulate a challenge that will survive examination. Fuzzy ideas can hide behind jargon – the addition of '-centric' was mentioned by an interviewee as one of their irritants. For example, 'We're customer-centric' – hmm, said the interviewee, if you weren't, you wouldn't have a business for very long unless you run a monopoly. The prevalence of jargon can hide a lot, so we need to focus on asking simple questions. *What do you mean by that?* is a question that isn't a direct challenge but which does require further articulation of the speaker's thought process. If there's jargon in the response, ask what the jargon means to the end consumer or customer: the question is easily justifiable if you say that, at some point, a team member will be asked to explain what the new idea means to them and their experience of dealing or buying from you. Asking questions also helps address the frequent mirroring that occurs in meetings. We often mirror the people around us to fit in, as we're not comfortable with challenge. Once again, there is a balance between a supportive and open way of working and one that gets railroaded by the dominant personality or the seniority of the person making the proposal.

Meaningless creativity comes from businesses focusing creativity where it isn't appropriate. Rather than spend two weeks coming up with ideas for a team retreat that encourages you to perform songs/improv comedy in front of colleagues (a process which can have its merits, but which needs trained input to stop it becoming a painful talent show in a random conference centre), examine where in your daily work practices or environment you could be better. Is there innovation that can happen in your processes, people management and development, the ways in which you communicate and engage your customers? Ask yourself: *Is this where we should be focusing all our talent and capability?*

There should be a discipline in your creativity. This might sound the opposite of what we're brought up to believe creativity is, but it is key. When reflecting on your ideas, think through the following question:

Can I explain this idea to someone who wasn't in the room on five charts or an A4 piece of paper?

This can seem to be hard. Three steps are needed: idea, implementation, results. If at any point you don't know the answer, you need to revisit your process. Ideas can often fail because they don't have a beginning, middle and end that hang together. A mantra can be: *If we do (a), we will need to have (b) in place to ensure that we deliver (c) as a result.* Creativity is meaningless when it doesn't produce the results you want. You are being innovative to create a meaningful change, not for any other reason.

The power of creativity for everyone

The power of creativity to empower people is enormous. If the organization that you work for operates in a way that means people do only as they are told, and don't feel that they can find their own way to solve problems, then there is enormous potential that is being unfulfilled. Talented people won't find it satisfying to work there and won't stay long. If you can inject a culture of creativity into the organization the upside will be huge.

Nick Lawson, Global Chief Executive Officer of media agency EssenceMediacom, is a firm believer in the upside of creativity to unleash potential. He reflects on working with a start-up creative agency, St Luke's, in the early 2000s. For a while, while working with them on an account, he was a frequent visitor to their London office. He remembers:

They had a classic, standard advertising reception. Then one Monday morning, when I arrived for a meeting, it was completely changed. It looked like a garden centre, with deck chairs instead of normal seating. So, I asked what had happened and why. The receptionist said that some staff members had decided to come in at the weekend and surprise their colleagues with the makeover. And I realized right then, that if you could have a company that cared that much, with people who felt empowered to do this, motivated to spend time at the weekend on this, and willing to put themselves out in this way, then there was an amazing culture and company.

Unleashing potential is, in Nick's view, the most important thing that you can do as a leader. He experienced this empowering upside when he ran a new business pitch, and one of the new prospective customers walked into the agency and immediately realized that they had left their bag in the taxi that had brought them. While the pitch ran, the Head of Reception, Sonya Biles, took initiative, found the taxi driver, and by the end of the meeting, the briefcase was in reception. In Nick's view she takes credit for that win. Every time someone takes initiative, it is an act of creativity.

Creativity therefore isn't just about making art or creating an ad or entertainment. It is about problem-solving. And problem-solving beyond analytics and pure logic, into a world where right and wrong are not black and white, where ideas are allowed to flourish and grow.

A comedy sketch by the UK comic John Finnemore illustrates this point. It ran on BBC Radio 4 and we overhear an English literature class. The teacher is increasingly frustrated by students with different opinions from him. He puts them down, he's sarcastic, but he cannot tell them they are wrong; after all, theirs is just a creative interpretation. Then the bell for the end of class rings, and the same teacher announces that because the maths teacher is away, he's taking the next class too.

'I'm afraid Mr. Pallister is away today, so I'm going to be taking you for maths. So, to start us off, who can give us the formula for the volume of a sphere? Uhm, Leonie?

Leonie: 2 pi r squared?

Teacher: No! No, it's not! That's wrong, that's the wrong answer! I shall tell you the right answer, which I know and you should learn! God, that felt good!'

The relief of the absolute, the fact that there is a binary choice in the maths class (right or wrong) when there was only nuance in the literature class, makes this teacher very happy. And surely makes lots of educationists happy too, as one of the biggest talks on the TED.com conference platform makes clear.

It is a very entertaining talk by Sir Ken Robinson, who argues that schools kill creativity. Sir Ken, whose talk is said to be viewed 17,000 times *every* day, argues that there needs to be a radical rethink in how schools cultivate creativity and nurture different forms of intelligence. He claims that little children aren't worried about being wrong about things, but that schools and businesses stigmatize mistakes. And if we discourage mistakes, we are discouraging creativity because if you're not prepared to be wrong, you cannot come up with anything original.

Remember what we said earlier about how confidence in creativity is lost as we grow up? Acclaimed science writer Annie Murphy Paul agrees that we routinely drain creativity out of kids so that we are left with grown-ups who are conditioned to subdue their creative instincts.

'Ask a group of second graders [aged 6–7]: "Do you think you're creative?" and about 95 per cent of them will say yes. Three years later that proportion drops to 50 per cent, and by the time they're seniors in high school it's down to 5 per cent.'

Both Sir Ken and Annie quote Picasso: 'Every child is born an artist. The problems begin once we start to grow up.'

It is also true that a standard education teaches you not to share your ideas (the very opposite of collaborating to create at work), and that there is peril to getting answers wrong – the kind of peril that ruins life choices. This book doesn't attempt to tackle education, but instead will show you how to tap into the well of creativity that we fundamentally believe still exists in every individual. You cannot actually drive the creativity out of human beings; it is absolutely innate. What you can do, and many businesses do, is discourage it from being used at work. Time and again, though, people who don't consider themselves in any way creative exhibit this creativity outside the workplace. Every tricky problem solved in their private life, every time they cook from scratch and don't follow the recipe book, every cake decorated, every special gift given with love, and every time they improvise their own words to a song that is half remembered, that is the creative impulse coming out. When you release that impulse in everyone in the workplace, you increase the power of potential exponentially. This book is your handbook.

Always on

Creativity is not a one-time, one-off, activity. Over the years we have, in various organizations, witnessed, participated in and even led creative thinking sessions. We have been trained in creative thinking. We have led training in creativity.

Frequently these have been enjoyable, entertaining, even useful. But more times than not they have been one-off sessions that are ignored once the business gets back to its usual rhythm.

If you're wondering what the point of all these activities was, you are not alone. They can be extremely useful as a way of giving everyone a good afternoon, or as a way to deliver a form of team bonding, making everyone believe (even if it is not really true) that they are contributing to the vision or direction of business. What these activities do not do is deliver real and empowering creativity. For this you need the culture of creativity to permeate the organization, and for creative thinking to be truly democratized and belong to everyone.

This doesn't mean that everyone who works for the business or organization is a creative genius, or that it is everyone's job to come up with a creative idea every day. But it does mean that creativity is embraced and welcomed, and that each time a problem is faced, or an opportunity presents itself, then creative techniques are used with a broad range of people.

In the current environment, innovative ideas are vital to ensure that your business survives. We cannot stress this enough. We are living in what are called VUCA times: Volatile, Uncertain, Complicated and Ambiguous. Let's face it, whether we like it or not, no one can predict what is going to happen next.

There was a trend around 2015–2016 for five-year planning visions – often called (because of the pun) '2020 Vision'. A selected number of 'key thinkers' were swept into a time-consuming workstream to invent the future. We guarantee that none of these efforts were worth the time, or the energy expended, because not one single business vision could have anticipated the global COVID pandemic, or the lockdowns and consequences that ensued.

Recent years are evidence that it is better to have a flexible, anti-fragile plan of action which can change given circumstances, than to waste time trying to predict the unpredictable.

So, baking real creativity into the workplace is the best way to keep the organization strong. Wanting things to stay the same, or to return to how they used to be, is as sensible a policy for growth and operational excellence as wishing on a star. The only constant is change, and the speed of change is accelerating – and the changes themselves are becoming less predictable than ever.

Creativity allows innovation. You literally cannot benefit from innovation without allowing imagination and right-brain thinking to drive developments and decisions.

Creativity also allows you to work smarter rather than harder. As AI becomes more prevalent, the winners at work will be those people who maximize the use of AI and develop new revenue streams, productive activities and sales strategies to make the best use of human talent while simple repeatable tasks are taken over by logic-based AI.

As you release people from boring tasks, you have the opportunity to reinvent what the team do with their time.

One of the main barriers to growth in business is too much muscle memory for how things are currently done. Even in organizations with very young employees, there is a huge tendency for stasis in this respect. People get promoted for being good at something, and they tend to employ people who are good at what they, as the boss, are themselves good at and value. So the team lacks diversity. A manager who values precision and analysis is normally unlikely to employ someone who lacks those traits. So, one way of working is perpetuated, to the detriment of the organization as a whole. And the ways of working get passed from generation to generation with no questioning of why things are done in this way.

Even when a new operating model or new practices are introduced, these don't tend to stick. Some people organize the training, other people are trained. Everyone takes time out of the day to day to be told how to do things differently. And then time and again they revert to the old ways of doing things. Habits are very hard to break. But if you want real change, you have to change how you work in the day to day. If you use the ideas in this book to deliver creative interventions on a quarterly or monthly or even a fortnightly basis, then the organization will change for the better. There are enough techniques in this book for you to try something new every week. This would revolutionize the culture of any organization. It doesn't necessarily mean that you would come up with 52 profitable ideas each year, and you probably don't need that many anyway. But if you regularly participate in creative thinking, you will change culture, increase happiness and inspire your teams.

As we will see, creativity can mean moving outside of your normal comfort zone. But this doesn't have to be extreme. In fact, we discourage extreme discomfort. The metaphor of sky diving to inject excitement into a normally mundane day-to-day existence is not what we recommend. Instead, we suggest that you and your teams step out of your comfort zones a little bit every week. As you do this the zones will increase in size, and brave decisions will become less difficult to make.

Keep an open mind, don't expect every experiment to work, and be clear that normal measurements might not be suitable for everything that you try. So many innovations sink because they aren't immediately profitable, or they aren't immediately embraced by the more conservative people around you. You need to be resilient in this respect, and if you believe in the new idea, don't be deterred by negative naysayers. If you are innovating, it is all too easy for people who are innately risk averse to argue against the new ideas.

Don't be swayed by this negativity. Creativity is undoubtedly the most positive and forward-facing activity that you can pursue at work.

It isn't something to do once a year and then forget about. Creativity should be always on; it should be a core part of normal activity, not a special event; and the more you practise it, the more the benefits will accrue to you, your teams, and your organization.

Creativity for the seasons

When creativity is always on, you can always resort to it to solve your problems and challenges. Once you have made creativity your habit, it is always at your side, always there to call on whatever the contingency. For small issues, or for a step change.

We have given working examples of 52 creative techniques in this book, more than enough for any business. The more they are used, the more useful they will be: uncertain times create unique barriers to growth, your creative resources will grow. Consider creativity as an extra muscle that just needs to be used more, and it will become a real asset to you. Like exercising any muscle, this might feel strange at first. But persist, and it will pay off. And if you have made use of some techniques in the past, remember that, just as you need to exercise your arms, core, and leg muscles, so you will find better flexibility and adaptability by trying different techniques. You will be giving them too to the rest of your team, and the gift of exercising creativity is one that nothing else can replace.

We list one technique for every week of the year and have classified them into the seasons for a year of creativity. However, we are not expecting you to use them literally for the seasons.

Our seasons are based on moods, themes and the rhythm of a classical British year (before the seasons became subject to the vagaries of the climate in the twenty-first century). And the techniques clustered in each chapter are themed according to those traditional seasonal characteristics.

So, we begin in spring. Spring is the era of radical change, of rebirth, of renewal.

These techniques and strategies of creativity concern themselves with big problems, where incremental changes are not enough.

Spring is an era of change: the days grow longer, the darkness of winter begins to be alleviated by fresh green shoots of growth. But the weather can be very changeable and challenging in its own way. The poet T.S. Eliot famously called April 'the cruellest month'. When the light grows and reveals problems, it can lead easily to despair. So, spring can be a time when you need to change direction. It also means nurturing the new shoots of growth, and allowing them to develop, while not expecting too much too soon.

From spring we drift into summer. The summer techniques and strategies for creativity are more about step-by-step change and allowing sunshine to help ideas to flower and shine. It is time to step away from logic. If you stick to logic, you are sticking to what you know you know. The nineteenth-century thinker Xenos Clark described logic in this way: 'we simply fill the hole with the dirt that we dug out'. In contrast summer creativity is about planting flowers, fertilizing growth, watching fruit ripen. Summer ideas are also about giving way to instinct, doing less, being lazy. Summer is about playfulness, piracy and fun. We will show how organizations can flower and be fruitful. Summer creativity practices are fundamental yet also joyful.

The theme of the autumn chapter is fall. It is about picking up after the fall, harvesting and rising again. It's about uprooting the old, about harvest and about new practices, new ways of doing things. When you find that the temperature of your organization has cooled considerably, when the leaves are falling and tried-and-tested practices are failing, then you need these autumn strategies. This might mean adopting new practices, reorganization of the entire team or the goals of the project. This process requires more than just a desire to change; so many plans of this type fail because workplaces are comfortable with how things are now. They usually reject the new in favour of *We've always done it this way*. In making organizational changes, there are steps to take in order to facilitate the adoption of new creative ways of working – by preparing the path to the acceptance of creativity and revolution. If you're going to get a new heart, you need to immunosuppress the issues that might make you reject this new chance of life.

Our final theme is, of course, winter. These techniques and strategies are about full transformation. Sometimes the toughest problems to solve need a complete transformation of creative approach, including considering new data or technology that hasn't been used in the sector before. This is the time to fire up the heat of creativity to thaw the ice of difficult and unrelenting permafrost or institutionalized barriers. There are situations when things need to get really bad in order for change to be facilitated. These solutions are dramatic, they are stark, and they will get results.

Although the format is seasonal – with the seasons corresponding to the type of creativity needed – it might be that you need a winter solution for a situation that takes place in July. If you are not sure which season of techniques are needed for your situation, turn to the end of the book now for a simple guide matching the season to common problems and frequent issues.

Above anything else the important point here is that there isn't just one type of creativity, nor is there one type of creative person. It is a complete myth that someone is either all business or completely creative and arty. You can, and you need, to be both to thrive in the workplace today. There isn't a choice between creativity and accountability, between innovation and heritage. At different times you need different resources.

In the next chapter we look at specific definitions of creativity from a wide range of creative practitioners, and how to prepare yourself and your teams to benefit the most from creativity at work.

CHAPTER TWO

Get ready for creativity

As we have said, many organizations are formed and normed for left brain, for order, for empirical decision-making. Where there is creativity, it might be regarded as fluffy, or elitist, and not subject to the rules of the real world.

As you take steps to drive competitive advantage through creativity, you must begin by getting yourself and your team ready to change, to be open and to create the conditions for success.

First of all, do a simple audit.

Audit what you have before you start

The start of the process for idea generation is key. Before you begin, you need to do an analysis of where you are, which people you can get into the process and how you can manage the workload and delivery of the idea and output. For this, we need to look at the type of people you could be working with as you create a new idea.

In his book *The Master and His Emissary: The Divided Brain and the Making of the Modern World*, the psychiatrist Iain McGilchrist examines how the increasing domination of the rational hemisphere of the left brain (the proof and facts side) over the intuitive side (feelings, creativity) has led to 'the banishment of wonder, the triumph of the explicit and with it, the mistrust of metaphor and . . . the cerebralization of life and experience'.

The right teams have an implicit balance between the left- and right-brain functions. The balance may shift during the life of the project, but you do need to have both. If you have a team full of left-brain people, you may not be able to make the big leap that is necessary to get to an idea. Their predilection for a bulletproof argument creates a situation where without proof, nothing gets done. While this creates a situation where all the concepts are robust, you also run the risk of never doing anything other than incremental change at a time when you might be looking for something radical and game-changing. This all sounds very obvious, but convincing left-brain dominant people that they aren't naturally gifted at generating big ideas can sometimes be a difficult task.

With your right-brain colleagues, the love of a big leap means they could have a tendency to follow the idea without considering all the practical aspects of their solution. They are the type of people who tell you that no one ever thought about snail ice cream until Heston Blumenthal made it a sensation, omitting to mention that the snail ice cream was available only at The Fat Duck, a restaurant whose customer base was orientated towards unusual flavours, and that no one has ever seen it at their local branch of Tesco. This isn't due to our friendly retailer not wanting to offer that flavour, it's because there isn't a business in it; the ingredients are hard to source at scale and there isn't a big enough market to make it worthwhile. Ideas are what you are looking for, but they have to survive in the real world. What seems like a wonderful notion after six hours in a hot conference room may suddenly disappear before your eyes at its first encounter with reality.

Another group that you may need to consider are those people who view themselves as the creative or idea experts. The 'big thinkers'. They are the ones who appear the moment a brainstorm or ideas session is announced, with Post-it notes and pens in hand, fired up and ready to go. They love whiteboards and at the first opportunity will be drawing a diagram to illustrate their insight. They can be very dismissive of anyone else with an idea or suggestion and can be hard to manage in meetings because what they prefer is their own, rather than the collective, agenda. It can appear that anyone else in the room is tangential to the generation of a new idea, as these 'big thinkers' are very adept at taking an agenda and making it fit what they want to do. It is tempting to include them in a team that is exploring new things, as they have the reputation for being creative. However, it's always worth considering whether they have that reputation because they have actually delivered a new idea that worked, rather than because they talk about their ideas and how creative they are. If you do include them, manage their input carefully to prevent them dominating the meeting to the detriment of any other participation or contribution.

The other area for consideration isn't around idea generation, though it is just as important to the process. When thinking about your team, with its mix of left- and right-brain thinkers (and carefully shepherded 'creative' people), you need a mix of inputs. This will, of course, be predicated by which areas of your company are needed to deliver and complete the idea, but the 'casting' of that input can be make or break. If you are taking a person from the finance team into the process, please don't let them be the participant who continually asks: 'How much is that going to cost?' before you have even got a workable idea. Of course, it is the function of the finance team to make sure we're mindful of what the costs could be and whether it's affordable, but be clear that at the ideas stage, you're not looking to create a full profit and loss analysis. What we need at this stage from our participants is the recognition that at this point it is only an idea – and not something to which we're committed. When asking for colleagues in different departments, be clear about what you're looking for, and if necessary, have a written brief. That way you avoid being told that person X was told by their line manager that their role was going to be Y and that's the only input they are willing to make. Clarity of both your brief and the expectation of participants in advance can avoid many issues right at the start.

A balance of enthusiasts and analysts can also be helpful. Enthusiasts can give you energy and momentum, but left unchecked will carry you away on the road to nowhere sensible. Balance them with analysts who can temper any wayward enthusiasm (and yes, we know that analysts can be enthusiasts; it's about knowing who is what in your team).

It might seem obvious in thinking about casting, but avoid any situation where there are personality clashes, an extensive personal history or even a close friendship. You need to avoid any sense that there is a gang within your gang, which can be excluding and negative for the work you are trying to do.

Ensure psychological safety

A 2022 McKinsey survey found that 85 per cent of executives believed that *fear* holds back innovation in their organizations. This makes it the norm. It is therefore unsurprising that most organizations do lack creativity and innovation. The antidote to this is psychological safety in the workplace.

It might seem like common human decency to ensure that people feel safe emotionally and psychologically at work. After all, health and safety in physical terms is a legal requirement. But people bring all kinds of emotional issues into the workplace, and it isn't simple to make everyone feel that they belong.

Our previous book (*Belonging: The Key to Transforming and Maintaining Diversity, Equality and Inclusion at Work*, with co-author Mark Edwards) looks at this issue in detail, and contains many detailed recommendations. As far as your team is concerned, it is crucial to remember that everyone brings their own baggage to the workplace. Sometimes one person's efforts for inclusivity can alienate another. This might be in the form of misjudged banter. One person might think their Monday morning jokes about what people have been up to at the weekend are acceptable camaraderie, but to others they are an unacceptable intrusion into their private life.

And many people, so many people, fear criticism.

This might be because of their upbringing, it might be schooling or friendship groups, but lots of apparently very confident individuals don't like the idea of failure of any kind. Not every creative idea is a winner. In fact it would be very beneficial if instead of the penalties for failing which are taught in school, children instead could internalize the comment made by Thomas Edison, inventor of the light bulb: 'I have not failed. I've just found 10,000 ways that won't work.'

Some of the most confident and extrovert people we have met in business are absolutely convinced that they are not creative. They have made their way by sticking to the proven facts and networking with others like them. These kinds of executives will encourage creativity in their rhetoric, they will even demand it, but only to be delivered by the kind of elite team that discourages it in everyone else. If your organization's leaders are like this, then they also won't take responsibility for creative risk and will miss the opportunities of innovation rather than face the consequences of things that don't work.

How, then, can you ensure that there is a level of psychological safety which means that ideas are welcomed, and innovation is embedded in the operating model of your place of work?

First make sure that you understand what is really going on with the people you work with. Remember no one intends to lose the advantages that come with creativity and innovation. People carry baggage with them, and we spend so much of our life at work that we can't fake how we feel there.

Some people have spent their whole lives trying to hide what they really feel, because their childhood experiences were that their true feelings were unlovable. They believed that if they showed how they felt, their parents or caregivers would be hurt or saddened. The author Robert Bly theorizes that everyone carries a long bag with them, stuffed full of those feelings and emotions from childhood which they learned were unacceptable at home, at school or socially. In *A Little Book on the Human Shadow*, he writes: 'We spend our life until we're 20 deciding what parts of ourselves to put in the bag, and we spend the rest of our lives trying to get them out again.' Or if there's just too much stuffed in that bag, it is likely to burst. For some people at work, the idea of free-flowing creativity is almost dangerous, as if it might lead to the bag leaking, and a side of themselves, their vulnerability, their fragility or their emotionality, might be exposed.

As a creative leader in your organization, you cannot expect either to solve this for everyone in your team, or to have a team where no one is affected by this sense of being stuck. Not if you're empowering everyone to be creative, that is.

But be patient with the idea that this is real for many and that you can't shake everyone out of it. Be gentle and be kind.

With this understanding, you can see past recalcitrance and perhaps diagnose vulnerability. Then there are many techniques you can adopt to encourage a sense of creativity and inventiveness among all the team.

Psychologists Linda Hartling and Elizabeth Sparks write that a healthy culture at work values 'growth-fostering relationships, mutual empathy, mutuality and authenticity to create qualities of zest, empowerment, clarity, sense of worth and a desire for connection.'

This won't be the case if there is too much hierarchy. If your organization does have a top-down structure, then create some regular creativity slots where everyone leaves their titles at the door and works together in a flat structure. Rather than ideate out loud, when the top leaders will end up judging output, use techniques to ensure that ideas are anonymous, and collected centrally.

Some cultures have become so 'nice' that no one can challenge anyone else out loud. This doesn't help creativity or innovation either. Hartling and Sparks call this 'pseudo-relational' where 'superficial niceness takes priority over constructive change.' This 'niceness' isn't really that nice because no one knows what is authentic – and everyone craves authenticity. Create instead a culture where it's safe to challenge and to make mistakes. This really needs to be led by example. As the creative leader acknowledge your own mistakes, shortcomings and vulnerability. You're not 'the daddy' or infallible. In fact, unless their job is presiding over the Vatican, no one in the organization is always right about everything. Some people might think that they would prefer to work somewhere where the leader is notionally always right. It might give them a sense of safety in a chaotic world. Gently bringing them out of this false security is better for them and the organization.

In addition, you must eliminate the sense that success for one individual is predicated on someone else in the team failing. There are too many workplaces that are entirely rigid in terms of promotion and success. When organizations start with ten people at entry level and explain on the first day that only five of them will still be there in two years' time, it doesn't encourage safe experimentation or any kind of psychological safety. Guy Kawasaki, author of *Enchantment: How to Woo, Influence and Persuade*, explains that there are two kinds of people and organizations in the world of business: the pie eaters, and the pie bakers. The pie eaters see the world of work as a zero-sum game. They are eager to eat as many slices of pie as they can because that means they are winning, and the others get less. Pie bakers have a different philosophy. They simply seek to bake a bigger pie. How? By being creative. Lift up your teams out of a scarcity frame of mind into a world of possibilities, innovation and creativity.

Get yourself ready

Personal preparation for creativity is really important. If you have the intention to bring creativity to the whole organization, you must prepare yourself physically and emotionally. You need to adopt a mindset that is open to opportunity, accepting of uncertainty, and of the calculated risk that innovation entails.

When things are stressful, remember that you have a simple way of de-stressing at your command in any moment.

Breathing, yes taking a breath, can restore your equilibrium. And an example of how powerful this technique can be is the fact that Michael Jordan used it. Author and mindfulness coach Mark Edwards describes it clearly here:

Michael Jordan, one of the greatest athletes of all time. Many would argue the greatest basketball player of all time. And therefore, a man who had enormous pressure on him. Every time he went out to play. He was the guy who was expected to win the game. To find that moment of genius.

He had a breathing technique to help him get from a place where that pressure might make him feel anxious or scared, and therefore detract from his performance to a place where he would feel calm, centred and focused on the moment.

The Michael Jordan breath goes like this. You breathe in for a count of four, you hold your breath for a count of seven, and you breathe out for the count of eight.

Now, if you do that – 3, 4, 5 times – you will find that you calm yourself down.

You know from experience that if your mind tells your body to calm down, it does not work. You have to get your body to tell your mind to calm down. And that's what this breath is doing.

You are slowing the breath down by holding your breath. We don't normally do that. And you're placing focus on the out breath. And by slowing the breath down and placing focus on the out breath, you are triggering a physiological reaction in your body…

… that says: It's okay to be calm now.

If it worked for Michael Jordan in the crunch games, it will work for you. In even the toughest business meeting.

Try three of them now.

(If anyone has any breathing issues, you don't have to do this. If you start to feel uncomfortable while you are doing it, just resume breathing normally.)

First just breathe normally. In. And Out.

Now breathe in -2-3-4

Hold -2-3-4-5-6-7

Out -2-3-4-5-6-7-8

Now repeat this three times.

You should find a quiet spot to practise this, but it won't take you long. You don't need more than a few minutes. We have ourselves taken a moment in the toilet facilities to steady our state of mind. But perhaps you can carve out a few minutes every morning or evening to do this.

In our experience, this never fails to be both calming and invigorating.

Taking a conscious decision to get into the right state of mind and centring yourself is as important to creativity as a warm-up is to an elite athlete. Just as you should never go into an exercise routine without doing a proper warm-up, in case you end up hurting yourself (and so won't be able to exercise at all for a while), so too you need to warm up for creativity or you might misstep. The consequences may be that either you are deterred from doing more or your team mutiny, disgruntled by stepping out of the normal routine.

You can think of this stage of preparation as *pre-ativity*, a conscious preparation for creativity.

In his book *The Tao of Bowie*, Mark Edwards references a book David Bowie was reading in the 1970s by the philosopher Julian Jaynes. The (still controversial) theory, outlined in the book *The Origin of Consciousness in the Breakdown of the Bicameral Mind*, is that until relatively recently the two sides of the brain operated separately. Edwards writes: 'In ordinary life, the left side of the brain handled things, but at times of stress their right hemisphere spoke to the left, giving it instructions on how to act. People perceived these utterances of the right hemisphere as coming from outside themselves. They were taken to be the commands of the gods.'

One way of thinking about pre-ativity is therefore a return to being open to accessing the insights of the gods, of the muses, of your own unconscious or of the collective's.

We're not suggesting you make sacrifices at any altar or consult an oracle. But you may need to find a way to silence your rational brain and allow illogical thinking to take you on a journey of discovering possibilities outside of the current way of doing things at your work.

The psychologist Carl Jung had a theory, seen by some as his most controversial, that as well as the individual unconscious (the part of the mind containing feelings and memories of which we're not aware normally, but which sometimes dictate our behaviour) there is also a collective unconscious. This is shared by all humans, containing archetypes and memories common to everyone, and developed over millennia. It's the explanation for some of why there are common myths and stories around the world in very different cultures – such as stories of a devastating flood, myths about dragons, the hero's journey.

If you follow this theory, then by gaining access to this collective unconsciousness you can access the creative instincts and ideas of humankind.

There's no proof of this concept, of course, and in fact it caused a rift between the two most famous psychologists of their day, Jung and Freud. However, undoubtedly, finding a state of mind where you can access unconscious instincts and feelings, whether they are personal or collective, can help you develop new ideas.

There are three words that are crucial as instructions for pre-ativity and creativity: Give It Time.

You can't hurry love, and certainly you can't hurry creativity. Let your mind wander, allow irrelevant thoughts. Accountability, either of output or outcomes, is not the enemy of creativity, but perhaps over-expectations are.

Your best ideas might surface during the creative thinking process, but they also might surface after the process, when you're no longer thinking about solutions (when you're exercising, for example, or in the shower). In fact, you probably need to make sure that you have a notebook or phone to note down thoughts that do come to you at random moments.

Once you've become practised at creativity, ideas will crop up all the time, as ideas from your creativity exercises, from your own unconscious or even from the muses collide, mash up and form into new and innovative patterns. So, get yourself ready for creativity by doing breathing exercises, allowing time for creative thinking, and being open to unconscious thoughts surfacing.

Four steps to pre-ativity:

Plan to give creativity the space it needs.

Get ready to defend the idea of creativity, but not to defend the specific ideas that you first come up with.

Be open to iteration, and re-iteration.

Take responsibility for creativity in the organization, and for following it through.

Research and insights

Hang on, you may be thinking, how does that very logical and sense-based concept – research and insights – have any relevance to the freethinking wildness of creativity, which can appear untamed by the restraints of cold, hard facts?

It's easy to imagine that the dissonance of these two opposing concepts would create two different forces of power, where you choose one or the other, and firmly plant your flag in the camp marked 'creative and freethinking' or 'insightful and disciplined'. Distanced camps, forever opposed and incapable of meeting in the middle. Never to coalesce or work in harmony.

We'd like to argue that this simplistic and rather naïve approach fails to grasp the possibilities that a détente between the two can help both sides. It's a peace agreement where everyone benefits and where, in their very opposition, you can find the power to create better, long-lasting results while also creating a narrative that means your success is capable of being reproduced.

Let's start with the basics of our research and insights. What questions are we asking? What is the purpose of the questions we are asking? Is it to find out where we are right now? Or is it to ask our existing/future customers what they want? If you know what they want, you can shape your offering to build yourself into the plans of your customers. Staying where you are, no matter how comfortable it may be, is perhaps opening yourself up to a number of future competitors taking advantage of your stasis. *If only* is one of the most frequently heard phrases in those organizations where there was a time when you could have kicked on and made change that lasted but chose instead the comfort of stasis. The innumerable excuses we make for staying the same – timing, capacity, budget constraints, lack of time to commit to change – are testament to our comfort in our staying in our lane.

So where does the logic come in? If we commit to asking the questions, we also need to commit to hearing the answers and then acting on them. So before we start our creativity push, let's think about the questions we ask at the start. These are simple and yet so often ignored. They are:

- Where are we?
- Where do we want to get to?
- How do we get there?
- Do we have the people to do that?
- Do we have the systems that can get us there?
- How deep and long a commitment can we make to this change?
- How much discomfort are we willing to live with during the process?
- When do we stop if we aren't making enough progress?

If you do end up stopping because you aren't making enough progress, you have more questions to ask, and only your insight into the process will allow you to identify them. This hindsight will, of course, offer a very clear view – and though painful, it can be informative.

When starting your research, be mindful in how you frame your questions. Make them too vague or nuanced and you're wasting your time asking them. Asking: 'How are you feeling right now?' is an example of this, as it's so open – *How am I feeling right now about what? The weather? My work? The music of Taylor Swift?* We saw this question in a work well-being questionnaire that was pitched to a few companies without framing it as a question asking respondents how they are feeling right now about work. The generous interpretation of this open question is that it allows each respondent to fully explain how they are as a whole, in order that their workplace can support them. The less generous interpretation is that a well-being organization asked the question as a way of selling itself. As a way to suggest that respondents who aren't in an optimal place, even if there is no realistic way for their workplace to address those issues, might benefit: 'X per cent of your employees feel unhappy, etc.' Use insight to provide insight, rather than to confirm a bias or act as a comfort blanket.

Start with your research, using this as a pillar for your creativity. It should be a framework for your creative ambitions, putting those endeavours on a solid basis. Knowing your customers – in full detail, where their ambitions and expectations lie – is your guiding light for creating a creative expectation. It is also worth thinking about researching your creative work as it develops, though do remember that there could easily be numerous examples of really great innovation that almost didn't happen because it wasn't warmly received in the focus groups. Again, this could be due to the nature of the questions being asked, or the context in which the research was placed. There is also a tension in bringing an idea into the spotlight of real people – the ideas generators accuse the audience of being biased/scared/incapable of understanding the work. This can be the case, but it may also be true that the creative idea is a confection that only works in the room where the idea was created. Exposure to the harsh light of reality can be very difficult. So be mindful of the tension between a brave, bold step plus the shock that boldness may bring, and the easy comfort of just making incremental change, which doesn't move you on enough.

During your creative process, research on your project can also be a source of insight and provide clarity. Going back to your first steps and charting your progress, can avoid an innovation that falls into stagnation. Ask yourselves: *Where are we on our journey? Are we where we need to be at this point? Are we still true to our objectives?* And the key question is: *Are we still in tune with what our customers want?* This final question is all too frequently ignored because we are so close to the process, and blinkered to the possibility that our own vision, rather than the one we had for our customers, has become our focus.

If you need proof of the crucial nature of innovation it's that it should be customer-focused, consider asking your friends which companies' innovations have genuinely improved their experiences and which ones haven't. We warn you that this may be a lengthy process . . .

What is creativity? A broad variety of views

People have lots of interpretations of creativity. As you have read, our focus is on delivering a step change of improvement in your workplace. During the course of researching this book, we asked a number of business people what it means to them. As you will see, their definitions of creativity are extremely wide-ranging.

Here's **Harjot Singh**, Global Chief Strategy Officer at the ad agency McCann & McCann Worldgroup (McCann was the 'real life' agency which featured in *Mad Men* as the chief competitor to Don Draper's Sterling Cooper Draper Pryce):

'For me, creativity is about seeing the bigger picture. And that's really about three things. Firstly, it's a way of being. It's not just a job function; it's not about what we do or make. It's just the way of being. It's also about questioning, not taking things at face value. And it's about drawing on my own personal well of lived experiences. If you can question things first, then you can reimagine them too. So, creativity is a muscle that allows you to take what life or a situation may have thrown at you and reimagine some new ways and possibilities to do something that serves your purpose.'

Claire Beale, founder of Creative Salon, which champions creativity in media and advertising, says:

'Creativity to me is a magical, alchemical thing, that happens when interesting people who look at the world in a slightly different way through a tilted lens, take something amazing that is in their head, that other people wouldn't think of and do something with it. I do believe everybody can be creative, and that creativity is a democratic process, but the people who are the most amazing creatives are slightly different to the rest of us. I love people who come at things with a different perspective and make me look at the world that feels like "this" rather than "that", who open your eyes, expand your horizons, make you feel excited about things. To be creative, I need jeopardy, a deadline that is already way past, pressure, somebody demanding something, a now or never moment . . . most of the stuff I do, in the moment of pressure and jeopardy, that is what I am most proud of.'

Tom Curtis is Executive Creative Director and an Instagram influencer (with one million followers) of the award winning 'Things I have drawn' account, which reimagines kids' drawings as if they were real. He believes:

'Anybody can come up with an idea, but creativity is all-consuming. Everything I look at I think, *Is there an idea there, is there an opportunity?* There're ideas, and then there's craft, how things are made.'

Stephanie Nnamani, the renowned visual artist, says:

'Creativity is a world between worlds, an unending carousel of curiosity, the most honest part of who we are. In creativity so much is revealed to us about the stories that we want to tell, the narratives that empower us, that we want to bring to fruition, and how we want to share that with people. There is nothing that comes close to how creativity empowers us and informs us about ourselves.'

Rory Sutherland, *The Spectator* magazine's Wiki Man columnist, and Vice Chair of Ogilvy and founder of their behavioural science practice, says:

'Creativity is the discovery of a destination that you didn't know when you started out on the journey. It's an idea that you can post-rationalize which is impossible to pre-rationalize. I suppose another way of looking at it is, it's the resolution of a conflict through unexpected or counter-intuitive means. Creativity to some extent involves just getting lucky, and the longer you leave it, the more likely you are to get lucky. Either new or unexpected information emerges or your subconscious somehow manages to solve a problem that your conscious brain is incapable of resolving.'

Tanya Joseph, chair of the Cherie Blair Foundation for Women and former MD of H & K, says creativity to her means:

'Problem-solving, using your imagination, to fix things. What you really need to do, how to do it, and doing it successfully. I spend time listening: to the radio, to books, to people, overhearing people on public transport, absorbing popular culture, soaking up ideas. I will have lots and lots of questions; what is the question that we really need to ask.'

Scott Morrison, the founder of The Boom!, and co-author of *Creative Superpowers*, says:

'I'm a firm believer that everyone is creative. As such, all we need to find are the right, tools, time, space and spark to explore it. Creativity is about joining up different dots in your brain and repurposing them to create impact. This happened to me during COVID lockdown. I applied the principles that I teach to all the people that I work with when I am doing creative masterclasses – but this time to my own business. I use the simple operating system I call Unblock, Unlock, Unleash. The challenge I had to unblock was how to transform my business during lockdown. I looked to unlock inspiration and ideas – I am a massive fan of stealing elegantly (someone else might have solved the puzzle you've uncovered) – go for a walk, focus on when am I at my most creative, and get myself into flow. That's how I joined the dots – finding hundreds of sparks, insights, ideas and turning them into new ways of bringing the Boom! But it doesn't stop there. The final element is about stepping ideas into the real world. That's where we Unleash our thinking and make the impact real. Ideas are cheap, actions are currency. Make something happen, get it out there, get real time feedback and constantly try things to create your own learn fast discipline.'

Eve Williams, General Manager at eBay UK, says:

'Creativity means thinking differently, challenging ourselves about how we think about things, and importantly, thinking about things that make it more interesting for our customers. That could be a conversation about challenging how we show up, how we manage our processes, how we use our data. As long as it allows us to have ideas that takes us beyond what we are used to, then we will get good outcomes. Creativity doesn't come from one person, or there is no single individual that is more creative than others. You need to listen to customers, to get inspiration from outside, look at the world, what is going on, to have conversations to collaborate, to think about what you're trying to achieve, but also to open up your mind to all the different ways it can be done. Creative ideas, as you shape them, can be uncomfortable; if we don't feel uncomfortable there is probably something wrong, and you're not being ambitious enough. Challenging yourself to make sure you're being ambitious enough is probably a good starting point.'

Zaid Al-Qassab, global CEO of ad agency M&C Saatchi, and former Chief Marketing Officer and Inclusion and Diversity Director at Channel 4, says:

> 'Creativity means things that spark emotion in other people fundamentally because they make people think of things in a new way or see the world differently.'

Sarah Jones is Director of Planning at Sky Media. She says:

> 'Creativity is problem-solving, in our jobs, and from a more personal perspective, creativity is about freedom, about being able to use your imagination to come up with something new and fresh and different that breaks the rules.'

Sam Learmonth, Global Art Director, says creativity is about:

> 'Mining possibilities and opportunities. Creativity is taking a few things that already exist, and plonking them together to create another thing. I write everything down and then it's like mining silver – you carry on mining [and] sometimes, there's more silver, sometimes it's just more mud.'

Neesha Taneja, Partnerships Director, says:

> 'I've had a long think about what creativity means. At its simplest it's making people feel something. It's intrinsically linked with emotions.'

Here's the view from New York-based **Anush Prabhu**, global Chief Strategy Officer:

> 'Creativity to me is an imaginative thought, brought to life, which changes or makes our lives better in some way'.

And to wrap up, **Vikki Ross**, copywriter, quotes Henri Matisse, saying: 'Creativity takes courage.' She adds:

> 'Being creative means being brave, not because we must be mavericks and do something big and outrageous, but because we have to think and do things differently, and to do that you must put yourself out there. Being creative doesn't allow a formula, it follows a feeling, so it comes from within, and it comes from our heart before it comes from our head. This is scary and takes courage. Even though thinking and doing things differently is scary, we do it anyway.'

A variety of views, and they are all, in our view, correct. It is a sign of creative thinking that views are divergent, and it is diversity itself that fuels creativity.

The necessity of diversity at work

Diversity of people at work is proven to help drive profits. Diversity of people drives innovation and creativity.

In the last decade, we have seen a drive to improve the diversity of talent in organizations, and a lot of research evidence for the specific profit metric has accumulated. In terms of gender, S&P Global's market intelligence team reported in early 2019 that companies with women as chief executives or as chief financial officers delivered more profit and drove share prices. In the 24 months post-appointment, women CEOs saw a 20 per cent increase in stock price momentum, while women CFOs saw a 6 per cent increase in profitability and 8 per cent larger stock returns. These results are economically and statistically significant. Companies with more culturally and ethnically diverse executive teams were 33 per cent more likely to see better-than-average profits, according to a 2018 study from McKinsey. In the UK, the potential benefit to the economy from full representation of Black and minority ethnic individuals across the labour market through improved participation and progression was estimated by the McGregor-Smith Review to be £24 billion a year.

Changing the balance of senior leadership in big businesses is a slow-moving issue. In terms of women running top companies, only 10 per cent of the Fortune 500 chief executives are women, and 8 chief executive officers are Black. There's a lot of training, human resources and culture policies aimed at this.

One of the reasons that diversity of people drives profits is that it also is essential for innovation and creativity. As we discussed in the last chapter, too much of a culture of consensus is a serious block to creativity and problem-solving. Like in any science experiment, you have to be willing to test a theory and find out that it won't work and why, as well as hope for successful experimentation.

Willingness to diversify is essential, and statistics suggest that outsiders can spot profitable opportunities that insiders may miss. One survey, of American business ownership in 2019 published in the New American Economy, stated that 22 per cent of business owners are immigrants, despite making up just 13 per cent of the population.

Outsiders are of immense value to your organization. They will bring challenges to the status quo which a highly bonded team might not, because no one wants to rock the boat. But it isn't rocking the boat that creates danger. It is complacency.

The story of how electricity transformed factories demonstrates this.

Up until about a hundred years ago, the new-ish technology of electricity failed to make much headway in business. The dynamo, or electricity generator, had been around since the 1830s. But until 1910, most entrepreneurs were still using steam to power their factories. Those innovators who did install electric motors were disappointed by the cost savings and efficiencies. According to the *Financial Times* writer and broadcaster Tim Harford, the reason for this was that most of them were simply replacing the steam engines with electric motors and using them to power the same factory processes. After all, this was the simplest way to update the factory.

But electric motors had the potential to revolutionize the entire factory process. Electricity can be safely and simply delivered wherever it is needed in a way that is not true for steam power – which must be generated from one central source of power. This meant that the old factories had to be arranged around the central power steam source, and were crowded, dark and dense. Steam set the pace, not the factory workers. Electricity is safer, cleaner, more flexible. To reap the benefits, however, the whole factory structure and the way everyone worked had to be ripped up.

Most factory owners were reluctant to change everything at scale and to sacrifice the old ways of working to new-fangled methods. It wasn't possible to run a small test and learn and reap the benefits gradually. For significant improvements, everything had to be reimagined. Old rules abandoned, hierarchies ripped up. Some expertise became useless. New experts emerged.

Eventually, decades after the invention of the dynamo, change came and factories hit new peaks of efficiency and productivity. The change was prompted by an external event, as travel from war-torn Europe meant more migrants and a radical shift in the availability of cheap labour and different kinds of expertise. This altered the dynamics of the economy in unexpected ways and redistributed skills and ideas.

It isn't just a person's origins, gender, sexuality, age, neurodiversity, specific disabilities or abilities that make a difference to your organization. The difference can also come from those people who just don't fit in. There are many different ways of looking at this.

One system that is widespread is *colours communications profiling*, which categorizes people into red, yellow, green and blue. Red is driven, strong willed, to the point. Yellow is people-orientated, emotional, outgoing. Green is empathetic, caring and careful. Blue is analytical, logical, detail-loving and questioning. All four types have strengths and weaknesses, good days and bad days. But the crucial point is that a mix of all four communication styles is better for creativity.

If your team are too much of one communications colour, then you are narrowing down the possibility of creative disruption. How can you tell? Well, if everyone in the team loves karaoke, or if everyone plays five-a-side football together, or participates enthusiastically in a charity baking competition, then you might have too many people of a similar type.

When Karen Blackett OBE, former WPP UK President and Chancellor of the University of Portsmouth, talks about diversity, she often mentions the importance of seeing diversity in top management as a key condition for ensuring everyone can be ambitious for the top. However, in her early career, where Sue first encountered her, leaders in the media industry were all white. When Sue asked her about whether this had been a barrier to her own progression Karen replied: 'When I looked up at the leadership, all I could see was a bunch of misfits.' Misfits who took that business to the top of its sector, and misfits who therefore encouraged other outsiders to develop and shine.

Outsiders – whether they are different in terms of origin, in terms of how they show up for work or in terms of personality – should be encouraged, treasured, valued and made to feel that they belong.

Create a pillar for the culture of your business

Creativity can be a real asset as a pillar of business culture. In times of great change and challenge, it can offer a new way forward. For the people in our businesses, it can energize their way of thinking and also drive closer collaboration between different business functions. It operates as a differentiator between competing organizations and can be used to deepen relationships between business partners and key suppliers.

No single company stands alone; it exists in a complex world that's full of interdependencies. With those interdependencies come a myriad of stakeholders in decisions and outcomes. *You want to change your product? Can your existing suppliers deliver what you need at the pace that you will need it? Or do you have to form new working relationships with another supplier who can do what you need?* All of this involves creating a partnership and capability where you get on with each other to achieve what you want. That means a new way of working will come out of your combined creativity. If it's new, then change must happen, and change is best driven by a creative approach to the emerging situation.

There is a concern that given how companies are run currently, it's only with standardization and simplification that we can get everyone to work the way that we need to be efficient. The problem with standardization is that it's just standard. We encourage our teams by having key performance indicators (KPIs) that are tightly controlled and monitored and which do, if managed efficiently, keep the status quo in place. However, in running those tight guidelines we remove flexibility in our response to situations and may end up as a faceless monolith. Having a voice recognition system for people who have a problem with a utility company output may seem an efficiency – until you realize that for people with speech difficulties, or whose first language may not be the one in your operating system, you are creating a barrier. If you are going to have a remote response system, then offer an alternative – a response bot on your computer to address the difficulties caused by having only one method of reporting issues. All too often the people who choose these operating methods don't engage with the wider teams that deal with customers and who are called in when there is no other alternative. Creative approaches would have possibly recognized the complexity of the situation that standardization doesn't.

In expecting consumers and clients to have only one response, we are reducing our opportunity to engage with them and make them fans of what we do. We frustrate and alienate our customers. They tell their friends (or take to social media) and the audience for their dissatisfaction multiplies. A niggle becomes a problem, a problem becomes an issue – and the whole thing just grows and grows. When working with Stamma, a charity that works with stammerers, we soon learned from their insights that the instinct to try and finish someone's sentences needs to be curbed – it disempowers the person with a stammer, and guessing wrong is frustrating for both. So imagine how this works in dealing with a call centre which has a set script and a set number of people – it just doesn't work. Thinking creatively about how you can support those groups is good for your business and your people.

Creativity also works in making our colleagues feel that they are building something bigger than their current role and that their input is valued. If we encourage and train our teams to be creative and give them the tools and tips to encourage and develop those capabilities, our team members grow and practise new skills. A company that invests in your training and encourages you to think differently is more likely to generate loyalty and commitment than one which just expects the same thing, day in and day out. If your opinion is valued, and your contribution encouraged, then you feel valued in turn. Frequently the reason people leave an organization is that they don't feel part of the company.

Incorporate business language for creativity

There may be a cognitive dissonance between business – traditionally viewed as hard-headed, fact-focused and logical – and the supposed wild thinking, unconventional ways of the creative world, and it may seem that this dissonance could not be more embedded. Creativity is viewed as emotion, ego and individual genius; business as teams, governance, guidelines and operational discipline.

In trying to bring those two seeming opposites together in harmony, can we assimilate the language of business to be more inclusive of creativity?

Let's begin with the much-used KPIs. Is it foolish to think that creativity, as pliable as it is, can ever be a performance indicator?

Perhaps if we look at the complementary nature of our usual business phrases alongside creative interpretations, we may find a way.

Key: What key elements do we think we can bring into the measurement of creativity? Initially, we could look at the numbers of ideas generated as we move our teams into a more creative way of working – just by having a period of time when any idea that could answer a business problem is given space, to encourage freedom of thinking and exploration. This is a signal of a shift in expectation and behaviour which a promise to be more creative won't achieve in isolation. It might seem at odds with the usual practice of a careful calibration of what is a key indicator, but perhaps we need to shake it up and relax a little with our language and positioning. Imagine how much that change of stance might induce in your teams. It may be that you ask for six weeks of *any idea is a good idea* just to kick-start the shift (despite the drawbacks discussed of this philosophy). That could be long enough for it to feel different without the senior team fearing that you have fallen into chaos. It also allows colleagues to be comfortable with a change and know that it is safe to explore. If during the six weeks you continue to have a risk-averse, *no ideas* culture, then have a long hard look at what could be holding those participants back and how you could do better next time.

Performance: What are we expecting? And when should it be achieved? Who else do we need to make our creativity blossom? Creativity is a team activity, even though we like to perpetrate the idea of the solo genius, who, blessed with a unique talent, is the only one who could have made this happen. Where would most respected artists be without the art galleries, art dealers and the audiences that appreciate the work? We could have the best ideas ever, but if we cannot persuade operations to allow us a trial session on something new, we are toast. Once again, we need to audit where we are as a business before we talk about the performance of creativity. Should we measure them in a way that recognizes where we are as a company – starting out on creativity, further along the path or fully embracing of a creatively led culture – before we even shape our performance expectations? *Yes*, we think, is the answer. Perhaps we might ask questions like: *How many of your ideas got to a discussion across disciplines? What are the next steps? Did the idea not land because of our own internal barriers? Or did a competitor get there first* (which means we have been sitting on the idea for a while)? These are the performance questions that we might be asking rather than the expected: *Did you do what we needed or not?* Or asking people to rate their creative output against an idea someone else had, which is never going to be an effective rating. If we are asking people to have ideas, they must have the freedom to fail – and the support to try again using what they learned from failure. Failure is rarely a welcome word in business language. We love euphemisms like *the outcome was not optimal* or *the circumstances around Project X were challenging*. They probably were but a modicum of honesty also helps: it shows you are not afraid to fail and that we all make mistakes. Sometimes they are even our fault. Right idea, wrong time. Bad idea, wrong all the time.

As in so many situations, there is no one answer that works in all circumstances. I have KPIs, you have OKRs (objective and key results). What works best? It depends. Language can be an enormous help in situations, but it can also be a barrier to clarity. If it is just a partner and myself running a business, would we use business language to address each other? Unlikely. We would have structure and goals – new clients, returning customer strategies – but would we have a full-blown corporate manner? Well, do you day to day? Complexity can be an enemy of creativity. Taking three pages of A4 to explain an idea might be a sign that it is too complex to bring to life. The way of executing the idea across the business might be that long, but not the one thought at the heart. The use of the word *heart* is also unlike the usual business speech pattern. We are not suggesting that you get emotional when you think of improvements to customer relationship management in Salesforce (or your chosen service provider), even though we are happy for you to do that if it suits you. You will use words like *efficiency* or *automation* around that improvement. In saying, *We are going to use this product to launch the very best customer engagement programme we have ever had, and this is the idea behind it* – that is a goal driven by business language and the idea of great customer service. The two can sit side by side.

Bring creativity into your business language if it works for you. Know your internal culture, expectations and timelines before imposing that language so that it can work as an effective tool of your creativity.

Hire and onboard for creativity

Remember that *butterflies in your stomach* feeling when you're about to start a new job? That heady mix of nerves, excitement and possibility? It's scary and yet thrilling, isn't it? There's no definitive point when that ends – depending on circumstances, it can be a few weeks or a few months, but that hyper-awareness can be a characteristic that you want to keep within your teams.

When you first join an organization, you're always asking questions and seeing where you fit in and what your role might be. You also arrive with a blank sheet of paper, with every possibility before you. It is a very creative time in your interaction with work. You have no 'usual' way of doing things and you bring a freshness with you. All too often organizations try to assimilate you into the usual ways of working and this can be a lost opportunity, for both the company and the employee. If you create an opportunity to use these fresh perspectives, it can feel as if you have received a bonus consultancy in new ideas.

Depending on the role, you may not feel that newness or creativity is needed. If you're in customer services, your job is clearly servicing customers – and yet . . . Give your customer services teams the freedom to use their initiative to address a customer issue. To provide a solution that's tailored and focused and which delivers to your client. That might not be the traditional example of creativity, but it is an example of how you view a situation and take a different approach. It can be as simple as offering a hotel umbrella to a client who doesn't have a coat when it's raining. The difference that makes – turning up looking good rather than soaked to the skin – is a bonus and a reason for that client to return. And for that client to talk about your customer care in a way that is more resonant than sending out a 'How did we do?' email after your stay.

When you're hiring, do you look for initiative or do you have a tick box of job criteria? Do you ask open questions that require people to think about what they could bring to the company? Would a small section about the problem or situation facing you and how they might approach it be appropriate or useful? It can also demonstrate how your prospective employee views your company, giving them an opportunity to avoid the same-y answers that you've heard before. Ask them: *What new ideas have you had about how you approach your role? What differences – even small ones – have worked? Have you had the chance to look at our work and what do you think of it?* And in the first few weeks, having a work buddy who can listen to feedback and channel any new ideas can be a great conduit for fresh eyes.

When you're hiring, think about adding a talent or perspective that you don't currently have. A new flavour to your fruit salad of talent, as it were. You wouldn't have a diet of just apples if you had the choice of other tastes, so why do we have a cookie-cutter approach to hiring? We keep taking the same approach, employing the same type of people and expecting the result to be different. To be hoping for a magical intervention or transformation is unrealistic at best and deluded at worst.

Let's imagine you've found your best-in-class candidate and they are due to start. How are you going to think about making sure they see that creativity is important to you? It's not decorating their desk in a funky way or organizing a welcome picnic and quiz night. That's great if you're happy to do that, but do be sure that the new person doesn't have something else planned for that night. Or hates quizzes. The first

90 days are said to be crucial in this phase of employment, so make sure you create the groundwork for a strong future. Psychological safety, where your new person knows that it's safe to ask questions, any questions, is absolutely key. Encourage them to follow up on any perspectives that might be useful, such as a new way of sector analysis, rather than assuming your way is the best way. During this period, encourage a wide-ranging programme of contacts, so that your colleague has a proper view of the whole of the company (and a wide range of people to call on when needed) rather than just the squad on their work pod.

Get them to take part in ideation, customer research, market analysis pieces and anything else that might stimulate them and bring their new and fresh views in front of others. It's key to make it clear that constructive input is welcome. Ask yourselves: *What can we learn from this person? What can we share with this person to make what we do a better way of working together, a better service, an improved product?* It's similar to when you have friends or family who visit your hometown and stay with you and ask to see the sights; you see where you live, where you have your own routes and routines in a new light. (Confession time: there are parts of London which we don't know very well but take it for granted that one day, when we have time, we will visit them. Fingers crossed.)

In this new infusion of personnel, let's treat this time as a fresh opportunity. This is particularly pertinent if you have a large intake of new people – apprentices or graduates, for example. A new perspective, not in the usual routines and with other minds to bounce off, can create real momentum. Why not ask them to look at some issues that might need exploring? It's also key that we give them the freedom that we would give to any outsider who comes to look at the company: the ability to speak without fear of the consequences and to have their opinions welcomed in a safe space. Think of it as a home-grown outside management consultancy project, which you can then nurture, incorporate and grow.

Fill everyone's bucket

Nurturing their creativity isn't something you need to do just at the beginning of someone's tenure with you. It is an ongoing necessity. If you and your team are used to following plans or complying with templates, you'll need to adjust to creativity. You cannot plan for creativity but you can get ready for it. Creativity usually will not follow a schedule, and you can't create a form to fill in to deliver it. You can open the door for it and get yourself and your team fit for creativity. In fact, this is essential. If your day consists of spreadsheets, commuting, chatting with friends and TikTok, then out-of-the-box ideas are actually less likely to come your way, or if they do, you're less likely to notice or take advantage of them. Just as you don't go from Couch to 5K without warming up and getting in shape, you can't expect brilliant creativity without some warm-up too.

You and your team need to get into training. The good news is that this doesn't necessarily take much time and it is fun.

Lives have changed since the last century, in that most of what we see or hear in the twenty-first century is driven by algorithms designed to deliver exactly what we want to see or hear, based on the last thing that we like, and inevitably, designed to drive revenues from subscriptions or from advertisers by growing audiences. The algorithms are just programmes that use data from where you're spending time and attention to suggest other things that you will like based on other people like you, and your history.

It works because a lot of the time we love things that are familiar or in tune with our existing preferences. Actually, sticking within the familiar was true for most people for most of human history. Most people (until the twentieth century, in fact) stayed within five miles of their hometown. And travelling abroad was for the rich and privileged, or for refugees. And of course, there was no rock and roll, no TV or internet and no cinema. So, it was a narrower world for most people in terms of interests and entertainment. A media environment that reflects back what you already love, that reflects those things which are familiar, is akin to human experience over millennia, and at the same time, is a straitjacket that keeps you within a circle of conformity.

However, this of course is not the whole story. We are curious by nature too, and seeking out cultural influences that are beyond our normal spectrum is both important and enriching. Anton Chekhov, the short story writer, playwright and physician, wrote in 1889: 'If a man knows the theory of the circulatory system, he is rich. If he learns the history of religion and the (popular) song "I remember a marvellous moment" in addition, he is the richer, not the poorer, for it. We are consequently dealing entirely in pluses.'

Therefore, your first task in order to prepare for creativity is to break those algorithms that think they know you better than you know yourself.

An algorithm is a mathematical set of rules specifying how a group of data behaves. In social media, algorithms help maintain order and assist in ranking search results and advertisements. On Meta/ Facebook, for example, there is an algorithm that directs pages and content to display in a certain order to ensure you spend as much time with the platform as possible. TikTok, Spotify and Instagram all work in the same way. The platforms want as much of your time as possible, and therefore go out of their way to serve you content that reflects your existing preferences.

This is not going to help you make leaps of creativity, or connections that are outside norms. So, for at least five minutes every day, do something unexpected. Go for content that wouldn't normally interest you. Buy a book that would surprise your friends to see you reading. Look at a magazine or website that is outside of your normal frame of reference. Meditate for five minutes, do some yoga or qigong, speak to someone you barely know, or haven't been in touch with for ages. If you usually listen to rap music, try some country songs or listening to Classic FM. If your favourite TV is comedy or *Strictly Come Dancing*, try a gritty documentary. Spend five minutes learning a new language or committing a poem or quotation to memory.

Then frequently – and we would suggest weekly if you have the time, but certainly monthly – take yourself slightly outside your normal comfort zone, and if you can, take your team with you. This might be a visit to an art gallery or museum. It could be a trip to a shopping centre where you don't normally spend any time, or to a film that isn't your normal choice. If you love live sport, try a ballet. If you love going for dinner in a good restaurant, try some street food. Go on an unusual outing, and yes, this can be fun, but think about finding unusual stuff as a priority over laughs. It really doesn't matter what you pick, so long as it feels like good food for your soul.

In 2013 the iconic, eccentric and world acclaimed designer Vivienne Westwood gave a talk at the Cannes International Festival of Advertising. She asked everyone to resist instant gratification and being 'stuck in the present' with no historical perspective. Westwood wanted us all to stop and think about 'the pursuit of our perfection', of always trying to eliminate imperfections in our lives. Sometimes life, and particularly creativity, is messy. She said that we all have an inner 'best self' and this – not authority figures nor celebrities, nor conforming to the norm – should be what guides and inspires us.

It's a great thought. We all know the difference between our best self and our ordinary self. The former can rise above our prejudices and look at the bigger, best, picture. Look to your best self for your recipe for bucket filling. What would [insert name here] do on their best day? That is the soul food to get you fit for creativity.

And check your circle. The British TV presenter and author June Sarpong has said that everyone needs to make sure that their circle of friends isn't only people who look similar, are of the same generation, sound the same and mostly agree with each other. Make this true too of your circle of inspiration. Seek out places, people and influences that surprise you.

One way to make this solid in the workplace is to encourage *reverse mentoring*. This means finding people who are different in age, origin or gender, or who would normally never find themselves together in any other part of their lives. Set some rules about how they should interact and see what comes of it. If it's done with openness and appreciation of difference, this should be mutually rewarding and encourage innovation.

If you and your team spend some time filling up your metaphorical buckets of inspiration, this will undoubtedly be time well spent. Get ready for creativity. In a world where so much of what we come across is driven by algorithms, machine learning and automation, a bit of escaping the norm is exactly what we all need. In the chapters that follow you will find many ways to do this.

So now, here are exactly 52 ways to be creative at work.

PART TWO

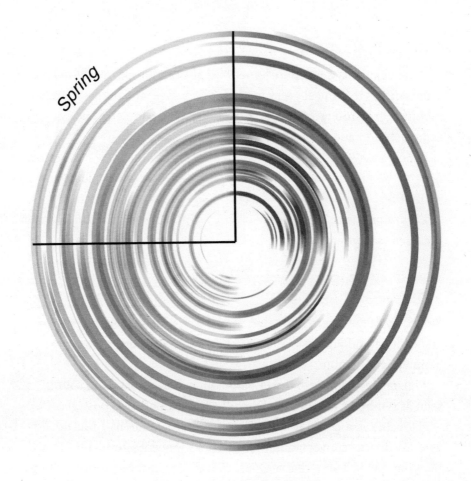
Spring

CHAPTER THREE

Spring – ideas for radical change

Radical change is needed in some critical situations, as we have seen. This requires looking at every workplace practice, and perhaps turning it on its head. You require everyone to have the courage to be open to every solution and to break with tradition and heritage.

When a new and unprecedented challenge is looming, this is the time to be creative using the techniques that we have collected for springtime.

Let's start with the story of one company who repositioned themselves from negativity to positivity for customers and employees.

McDonald's: taking the Golden Arches global and local

How do you take something that is so intrinsically American – with its associated good and less welcome elements – and turn it into a casual eating phenomenon?

McDonald's is more than a fast food outlet. Their arrival in a country is seen as symbolic, as when McDonald's opened in Russia post-glasnost. McDonald's is a cultural icon. The film *Pulp Fiction* had McDonald's as a recurring conversational element – Vincent's revelation, while hanging out in Paris, that a Quarter Pounder is called a Royale with Cheese makes a few appearances. It even leads to a discussion about the metric system. Clearly Quentin Tarantino thought that the inclusion of the Quarter Pounder added something to the idea of an all-American perspective being filtered through another lens.

McDonald's has faced some difficult times. Its competition is never-ending as our culinary tastes become more global. In the UK, since McDonald's arrived in 1974, there are now a multiplicity of casual dining options from pizza to sushi, Thai to Poke, Indian and Vietnamese (and that's just the first glance at the local guide). So how did McDonald's reinvent itself to stay ahead? What lessons can we learn?

Facing into a crisis is sometimes the point where creativity and forward thinking just stops. Not long ago, McDonald's had a series of major issues, all in a relatively short time. *Super Size Me* was a documentary released in 2004, directed by and starring Morgan Spurlock. It follows a 30-day period where all Spurlock ate was McDonald's food. The film documented the effect of this diet on his physical and psychological health.

McDonald's had already faced consumer concerns about the provenance of the ingredients it uses and the quality of its products. Coupled with this, high-profile individuals were questioning the prevalence of takeaway/fast foods and asking how these were contributing to obesity and poor health outcomes.

So how do you make your customers, and your employees, love and trust you again?

McDonald's knew they had products that customers loved. Now, under scrutiny, they redesigned nutritional profiles. From the start they had high standards. Anyone who is connected with marketing McDonald's, even from outside suppliers, is expected to work for a week in a restaurant so that they fully understand how the company works. From Managing Director to the newest trainee, if McDonald's is your client, you do your stint. There is no excuse (and it's a great way to get people to understand what you're doing to deliver to the customer).

One of the strengths of McDonald's is that you get the same product everywhere. But this had become a negative as well as a positive. Creative thinking at McDonald's led them to recognize that they could build on the core product but make it local. Yes, you'll get a Quarter Pounder, but there's more than just the *Pulp Fiction* name change going on. McDonald's in New Zealand offers a Kiwi Burger, which is a burger with the addition of egg and beetroot. In Brazil you can get Banana Oven Pies. In Japan, teriyaki burgers are available. Should you find yourself wanting something unusual in Germany, try the McCurry Wurst. It's a take on the traditional German sausage. The management recognized that to build affection in audiences, you have to be part of their lives and identities, and therefore that you need to localize your approach.

Are you taking a one-size-fits-all approach to your consumers? Is there a value in some tweaks that make your target market feel that you 'get' them and what they want? By listening to your consumers, you can create a product that means something to them. Do you talk to your customers about what's important to you, rather than what's important to them?

In the UK, McDonald's today has a tone of voice that they describe as 'confidently humble'. Essentially, it's a combination of being humble combined with self-assured simplicity. No arrogance or posturing, just being sure of what they say and how they say it. Quite often, communication fails not because of what is being said but because of the way it is said. It's how you make people feel when they hear from you that resonates, rather than the detail of the content. However, UK marketing for McDonald's had become increasingly offer-based and short-term in terms of return on investment (ROI). It now decided that rather than being driven by short-term promotion to promotion, one event after another, they would focus on being trusted and loved.

In marketing terms, this was a positive and radical creative intervention.

Love and trust are hard to achieve, and there isn't the instant gratification of a three-week push on a specific product or giveaway. However, love and trust bring loyalty and people talking about your brand or product in a positive way, and in a world where it's hard to gain attention and traction, that is worth a great deal. Love and trust requires a long-term commitment to telling that story.

You will get it wrong from time to time – everyone does and it's almost inevitable when you're taking an emotion-led approach. It's the rituals and behaviours of being in McDonald's that give it resonance. (Our friend Mark can talk about McFlurrys for longer than you would believe; the man is an expert. The fact that we have never had one is a source of astonishment to him.) The key element of creativity in this approach is to know where you've made the mistake and not repeat it: learn and move on.

Based in 100 countries and with 36,000 locations, McDonald's is massive in both size and scope. It has faced a huge level of ever-evolving and varied competitors and challenges (the growth of delivery services, COVID, changing consumer food preferences and fragmenting audience sectors). Its creativity lies in a tone and approach that is embedded in the company and the way that it operates. It has its end customer at the heart of everything it does. It's not afraid to tweak its core product offering to make it resonate with the audiences it serves. It wants to be loved and trusted by its consumers while focusing on giving them value. The step change from selling fast food at a discount, to investing in creating love for the brand is a good basis for creatively developing your business. The team push for fresh ways of reaching the hearts and minds of their customers, and insist on pushing for opportunities for growth even when times are hard.

Here are 13 techniques to help you with radical positive change. Spring creative techniques are all about finding joy in new ideas and approaches, and could give you the opportunity not just for personal and emotional growth, but for creative ideas that can create breakthroughs at work.

Push the idea till it breaks

Start a revolution

Use new

Exaggerate

Be brave

Allow time for shoots to flourish

Double the resources available

Prompt the unconscious

Change direction

Make it iconic

Give it purpose

Random link

Spring forward and be more *dog*

Push the idea until it breaks

Sometimes we need to be reasonable. Sometimes we need to push, and then push further. When we do, we might get something we did not expect.

Musicians have a long history of altering the sound of their instruments. The earliest preserved guitar had just three strings and was found buried with the Egyptian singer Har-Mosĕs and his plectrum close to the tomb of his employer, Sen-Mut, architect to Queen Hatshepsut. Since then, the shapes of guitars have evolved, and many strings have been added.

Arguably the most exciting development came 3500 years later in the 1930s, with the production of the electric guitar.

The Rickenbacker 'Frying Pan' was created in 1931. The solid body electric guitar, which really transformed popular music, was introduced by Les Paul in 1941. Les Paul recorded as many as six musical parts on 1940s' tracks, and designed and built his own multitrack tape recorders.

But the real sound of modern rock music belongs to distortion – deliberately pushing the instrument to and beyond its limits. In the 1950s the sound of the guitar evolved based on sounds created earlier in the decade by accidental damage to amps: for instance, 1951's popular recording 'Rocket 88', by Ike Turner and the Kings of Rhythm, is considered by some to be the first rock and roll record, and its unique sound was created when guitarist Willie Kizart used a vacuum tube amplifier with a speaker cone that had been damaged. Then, in 1962, a Nashville engineer named Glen Snoddy invented the Maestro Fuzz-Tone, which took the natural sound of the guitar and distorted it beyond recognition. This is the sound of modern rock. As guitarist and historian Tom Wheeler writes, 'If you're Keith Richards and you're doing 'Satisfaction', you could play that line on a clean guitar, but it just would not have that in-your-face, gnarly, dark quality that has so much attitude to it.'

This heritage of pushing beyond what is normal has continued with the autotune. Created in the 1990s to help correct singers who had sung off-key, it has become a sound in its own right. The original intention was to help save time and money by ensuring that you could correct any recording where the singer had been out of tune. However, autotune turned up to the max created a new sound for singers, which has entranced the pop music market. Cher used the futuristic sound on 'Believe', which became one of her biggest hits, and even now the distinctive autotune sound is known as the Cher effect. These days everyone uses it, either to enhance a natural voice, or to transform a sound. Top artists using autotune have included Daft Punk, Rihanna, Britney Spears, Black Eyed Peas, Kesha and Drake. It's now the sound of all modern pop. And it might make you wonder why you, yourself haven't recorded a pop song. After all, you don't need to be able to sing in tune.

These are two innovations that took perfectly beautiful sounds – of classical guitar and the human voice – and distorted them to the point of breaking them, and thereby created something new.

Take Action

Push your idea until it changes, breaks and becomes something new. Don't stop coming up with ideas when you think that the answer is good enough. Push harder. Break the category or product norms. Don't worry, you can always roll back if necessary. But you just might create an innovation that changes the world.

Start a revolution

According to a McKinsey survey, 94 per cent of executives are dissatisfied with their firm's innovation performance. It's enough to make us all hand in our passes to the brainstorm meetings and sprint sessions, and just head home for a nap. After all, it appears that none of the existing methods are working, so why bother?

Perhaps it's time to have a revolution, so that there is more than 6 per cent of executives who feel satisfied with innovation.

Start from the basic observation of whether your day-to-day routines and rituals are holding you back from the creativity that you need. Should we change the way that we approach our future plans? Look at who is in the room and see what their role is, and consider changing the hierarchy so that the meeting is run by a relatively junior person who may bring fresh eyes to the problem. In this situation there is also the advantage that no one is worried about what a 'wrong' idea might do to their promotion prospects.

Do you always hold your sessions at the same time, in the same place on the same day? Change it up. Break down your problem into different sectors – target clients and what they say they want (and what they don't say), operations, delivery and logistics. Then get smaller groups to go out for a walk, have a coffee and think widely around the issue. Nothing is out of bounds in these smaller groups. It's when you bring the ideas together that you can collectively knit them into one; now isn't the time to delve too deeply into tiny detail. Revolutions are big, as well as a little scary, so let's embrace them fully.

Revolution succeeds only if it's wide-ranging (otherwise it's merely a pressure group). Collaborate widely across and beyond your organization to create your plan and process. There are many cases of people seeing one small way of working in another sector that made them reappraise and review how they did things. Don't be someone who blindly assumes that you know it all.

While you're having your revolution, the dismantling of your hierarchy might be uncomfortable. However, if you don't embrace the revolution, the fear of raising questions or the fear of any repercussions from dissent acts as a brake on truly forward thinking. It's safer to stay the same with the focus on predictable, reliable results – but you'll gradually become one of the many, many places that wind down into full-on inertia and irrelevance.

Insist that at every meeting there is only a basic summary of where you have got so far, with 90 per cent of the time spent on moving forward, pushing the idea or proposal so that it can become bigger, better and bolder. Don't worry about a six-month KPI target. This revolution has to excite and change what you do. Changing the typeface of the packaging isn't going to make your target audience rush home to share the news with their loved ones. Unless they really love typefaces, that is, or have no other news to share at home.

Start from the impossible and work backwards. Stop before you get to where you are comfortable. You are already comfortable (and that's why 94 per cent of executives think innovation levels are unsatisfactory). Ban the word *incremental* from your meetings.

Also consider whether the word *alignment* has any place in your revolution. (Hint: it doesn't, because no revolution ever was built on people being in total agreement.) Allow in a little tension and see where the exploration takes you.

Take Action

Work out your rules and turn them on their head. You need to understand what the heuristics, or rules of thumb, of your category are, and then break them. Write a list of the conventional wisdoms and then a second list where you do the opposite of what is on the first list.

Use new

We all like familiar things at least some of the time. The daily rituals of everyday life. A favourite mug, a regular walk, the autopilot of the normal commute to work.

The creativity training company ?What If! calls this staying in your stream. In their book on innovation at work, published in 1999, they talk about breaking the pattern to which our brains default. Human brains make shortcuts and rely on previous experiences in order to make decisions fast. ?What If! says, 'On average we put on seven or eight pieces of clothing each morning. Imagine if we had to try each one out every time to find out where it fitted best . . . . There are over a million possible combinations. Fortunately, our brains don't bother us with all those possibilities. Instead the brain simply says, "that looks like a sock, it'll go on your foot". The brain leads us to make assumptions that if something is familiar, if you know where it goes automatically, then you won't challenge this.

This is where conventional wisdom wins. Every time you try to break conventional wisdom, you'll find resistance. First from your own brain – every instinct might be screaming at you to conform – and secondly from everyone else's similar reaction. The more there is conventional wisdom surrounding you, the less likely you are to come up with an innovative and creative solution. In fact, you may keep everyone around you happy precisely because you aren't challenging the status quo. You are very unlikely to make them happy because of your innovative solution to any ongoing or new problems.

Embracing the new is crucial for growth, and one way of ensuring that you do this is by trusting new people, and those who lack experience but bring fresh outlooks.

Arsène Wenger OBE was the longest-serving, and most successful, manager of Arsenal Football Club, a football team based in north London. Appointed in 1996 he was at the helm during a celebrated period of successes including trophies, unbeaten runs (42 league matches without defeat) and participation in the Champions League in Europe. Football managers usually don't last long in England – the average tenure is just a couple of years. Wenger remained in role until 2018. And he did so by embracing the new. As well as making changes to training and diet regimes (out with junk food, in with boiled chicken and vitamin injections), Wenger was famous for backing youth.

Over his 22-year stay in the role he cultivated raw talent and emphasized the importance of training and scouting young kids. He regarded trusting youth as one of the key values he brought to the club, saying: 'We want to be very successful without neglecting the need to give a chance to people.'

Rich clubs had a tendency when Wenger took over to buy in talent that had proved itself already in another club. Wenger prioritized investing in youth instead. So much so that Arsenal became a feeder club to bigger teams. But he found and developed dozens of young players, including Patrick Vieira, Bukayo Saka and Robert Pires. The Youth Academy he set up is one of England's most successful and many of the players sponsored by Wenger are still playing at the top level.

Who have you got in your youth team at work? When a role comes up, can you promote someone into it who is short on experience but long on potential, and give them extra coaching and pastoral care? It's possible that the lack of experience and understanding of *how we do things round here* will lead to better ideas and new breakthroughs.

Take Action

Use new people to add challenge to solutions that you are defaulting to. Bring the outside in, and don't wait for people or ideas to prove themselves before you try them. Introduce naïve or inexperienced team members and listen to their first impressions.

Exaggerate

Take an idea, take a problem, take a question and exaggerate it to help you find a creative outcome.

One of the most iconic pieces of advertising did this beautifully. The Sony Bravia ad featuring thousands upon thousands of colour balls bouncing down the streets of San Francisco took the literal idea of enhanced colour and exaggerated it into something that would not just transform your TV experience, but which would transform your whole physical and emotional experience. The art director Juan Cabral reportedly wanted to exaggerate even more than the final shoot allowed; he wanted to throw a million balls through the streets. It turned out they couldn't find a million balls in time for the shoot, and so a mere 250,000 were used.

Apple's '1984' commercial presented us with conformity exaggerated into a dystopian nightmare, relieved only by Apple's revolutionary new computer.

Old Spice offered us 'The man your man could smell like . . .' Not really, of course, but yes in your wildest dreams.

Beyond the realm of advertising, exaggeration can drive creativity. *Peaky Blinders* writer Stephen Knight took the real lives of a Birmingham street gang and exaggerated the characteristics of one gangster – Sam Sheldon. But by making him smarter, prettier and more heroic, he created the show's magnetic protagonist, Tommy Shelby.

Exaggeration of threats can lead to creativity in business problem-solving. This might seem unnecessary in these times of change and disruption, but change is less difficult if you can get ahead of it. Reimagine customer service by auditing best in class service, not in your competitive set only but beyond the sector where you operate. What would happen if your closest competitor delivered at that level? What actions do you need to take now in order to ensure competitive advantage?

Risk management requires not only imagining the worst that could happen, but also working through the business's appetite for risk, should the worst occur.

New product development and increased satisfaction can be accelerated when you pre-empt a potential client or customer re-pitch by offering a solution to a problem that the client isn't even aware they have yet. How about imagining the client in question as the most unreasonable client you've ever met? Consider them to have the standards of the princess in the story of *The Princess and the Pea* and the patience of a toddler.

In 2020 one of your authors was engaged in a global advertising competition. As part of a team who were answering the brief for the Cannes Lions *Creativity for Good* competition, we applied exaggerated thinking to one of the insights. Francesca Ranieri, one of our teammates, noted that 'if women received as much business funding as men, and if they combined their business worth, they would become the most powerful economy in the world.' From this exaggeration of the economic facts, with fellow team mates Luka Mavertic and Ifeanyi Dibia, we developed the award-winning campaign to create endorsements for products and services Made in IWON (International **WO**men's Nation, an imagined state) for the World Woman Foundation.

If you are having a tough time, creative exaggeration can be surprisingly helpful. Is there something you're dreading? A difficult meeting? A speaking engagement? A networking event? What is the worst thing that could happen, and if it did, how bad would that actually be? One of the authors has a genuine fear of networking, which has been resolved by support from her co-author and also inspired by asking her brilliant daughters how they were so good at networking (even from a young age). They replied: 'We just think, if it goes badly, we don't ever need to speak to that person again.' Cognitive Behavioural Therapy includes this technique too as a way to stop worrying – exaggerate to the worst-case scenario and then go further and work out what your reaction might be to that. According to *Psychology Today*'s 'CBT made simple': 'If the worst case scenario were to happen, what would you do to cope with it? If you do have a bad meeting, you might be disappointed for the rest of the day, curl up on the couch with some ice cream and watch TV. Then get back on the horse the next day.' Creative exaggeration can help with all kinds of scenarios: imagining the most extreme vision can be really useful.

Take Action

Looking for a creative solution? Exaggerate, be dramatic, turn it up to the max. Look for the most extreme version of events, and be bold enough to follow it through. If the London Olympic opening event organizers had thought too hard about approaching Queen Elizabeth II to participate in the gala, they wouldn't have – and not only did she participate, she let herself be escorted to the Olympic stadium by James Bond and then 'jumped' out of a helicopter.

Be brave

Bravery at work can be a complex subject and the majority of people aren't comfortable with the idea. Is bravery only about confronting injustice in the workplace? Not necessarily.

By encouraging our teams and colleagues to be brave, we encourage risk-taking, which in turn leads to innovation and new ideas. As we've established, creativity is key to the advancement of an organization and if employees feel the courage to ask questions, speak up and try new ideas, the innovation is more likely to be based in reality and to take root as a method or approach. It also makes colleagues feel that they have an input in the future of the place where they work.

We have talked earlier about the drawbacks of brainstorms, but if you are going to hold them, at least stick to the rules you give people. We have heard stories of sessions where the organizer says: 'This is a creative space, there's no such thing as a bad idea', swiftly followed by: 'Except that one, Joe' to the first notion that raises its head. Yes, it's a dreadful example of behaviour and laughable in its restrictive approach, but are your sessions structured in a better way? Who leads them? What's their way of working? Is it open and encouraging or dismissive and defensive? Think about the questions that you are asking, the way you handle suggestions and give feedback – and be brutal with yourselves.

We have heard of a management session in a business where the top tiers of the business were taken away for three days to a very expensive hotel and asked to come up with three ideas to change the company and make it market-leading. The exercise was not set up in the right way – the cross-vertical teams created had no real knowledge of how the other businesses worked or their strengths and weaknesses, so time was wasted in explaining why certain approaches wouldn't work. The reasons were regulatory, geographical or logistical. Everyone knew a lot more about the business by the end – but just asking for three ideas, with no context, knowledge or process, was bound to fail. Even though the teams did have ideas for the final session to the board, not a single one was ever explored beyond the confines of that three-day strategy session, and where there should have been feedback there was a void.

We're not suggesting that your sessions become a free-for-all, with no structure or process. That is simply wasting time and not appropriate. However, in creating a clear structure you stand a much better chance of success. Think about your language and approach. Saying: 'That idea is clearly nonsense, Janet' will not make Janet the most vocal of participants next time around. How about a new language? Not *yes* or *no* but more encouraging? You could group your suggestions under three headings:

Pause – an idea that might have merit, but currently isn't as viable/ within your capabilities.

Polish – an idea that looks interesting at first glance, so what more do we need to do to get it to the sweet spot? Are there operational, logistical or other elements we need to consider before taking it to the next stage?

Perfect – an idea we love, so how do we make it ready to go?

The main drivers for people not being brave are the fear of criticism and consideration of career progression. Encourage your colleagues to talk about their ideas for both strength and weakness. While they are doing so, don't allow a feedback loop that kicks in immediately. It's not fair. Let the whole idea play out and then use phrases such as *'That's great, it could be even better if . . .'* By encouraging people to be brave, we also give them more agency in the organization and sometimes it's the people who do the job day after day who recognize that a process developed at arm's length is never going to work.

Take Action

Create psychological safety to ensure that the whole team can be brave. Start each meeting with the reassurance that this is a safe space. Tell a personal story about bravery, and making a good mistake – the kind that we can all learn from.

Allow time for shoots to flourish

When we are using creativity to drive change, it's usually driven by business considerations wider than just a desire to do things in a new way. Your organization may already be acutely aware that its competitive advantage is losing its edge, or you may be in the chasing pack that wants to catch up with a competitor. Going through a process of refreshment because you're becoming conscious that you're in danger of becoming stale can also be a consideration. Refreshment can sometimes be the hardest process of all, because the team might feel that nothing is wrong, that customers are happy and that you're hitting your numbers, so why is there a need to do anything now?

Creativity has to be welcomed within teams or it won't have the desired effect. You need it to take root in the culture of the organization and be seen as a welcome part of your way of working. A series of tweaks that are viewed as meaningless and unnecessary is damaging, even if it isn't causing any major issues. So how do we create the conditions for creativity and ensure that what we do isn't a pointless exercise in blue-sky thinking?

Frequently, the exploration of the new is framed as a need to find a fix. Just the one fix or perfect answer that will be the solution to present and future issues. This is an approach that can throw up a number of issues in itself. Firstly, the notion of the ultimate goal puts a huge pressure on the process of creativity due to the intense focus on getting to the right idea at all costs. That level of intensity can make participants in any creative process feel that only a fully formed and ready-to-use solution is needed. It's rather like being asked, unexpectedly, to tell someone your favourite joke. Very rarely is the response a mirth-inducing quip that hits the spot. Under pressure, most people just say they can't think of one right at that moment, making all participants in the conversation feel slightly awkward – the person who asked for the joke wonders why they bothered and the person asked is left flustered and feeling helpless. Pressure might seem like a fix but normally it isn't.

When we are trying to solve a problem, it can seem that having one focus is the best approach. However, we would encourage you to allow more than one strand in process, so that you can have a number of options in hand to spread your risk. Armed with our ideas and a pathway to develop them, start your process and let the teams involved take their time to analyze and road-test their approach. The process is like growing plants – you plant the seed of your idea, you nourish and water it and then you wait. Interestingly, the first shoots that pop their head above the ground might seem like the strongest, but sometimes the opposite is true: they have emerged too early and a change in conditions can be fatal. (For plants it's frost, but for ideas it can be that the initial approach doesn't survive the brush of reality.) Give all of your shoots of creativity the chance to take root, and then see what emerges.

The other benefit of the multiple, considered approach is that you allow a wider section of the team to play a part in the development of an idea. All too often creativity is seen as a specialization accessible only to an elite, more able set of people. This is not the case. Most calls for creativity aren't focused on creating the Sistine Chapel of business, right? So, give your colleagues the free rein and the confidence to grow their ideas. The time will come for you to plant out your ideas, but in the interim let them start the journey to blooming.

Take Action

Nourish your ideas as if they were spring seedlings. Protect them from frost and keep them watered and warm. Allow them time to flourish. Don't go straight to the negatives. Avoid too much criticism and keep mulling over the thoughts to let them develop.

Double the resources available

Unless you're part of a large organization that has the luxury of your own research and development unit, which even then can be focused on just one part of the innovation within a company, you're probably trying to be creative while doing your day job too.

This can be one of the reasons why people resent being in sessions aimed at future-proofing the business. It's all great for the Financial Director to be talking about the company and its prospects, but all you can think of is how your mobile is currently ablaze with calls from a customer whose order hasn't turned up – again. It can be hard to be creative when you are fearful of what storm is brewing. When allocating resources, be mindful of the pinch points in the areas you're asking to help. Financial year end, summer holidays, trade shows – it might sound obvious, but these resource black holes are often forgotten.

Creativity can come out of adversity, but desperation is not the ideal starting point. If you are setting out a path to change and develop, it's essential to have a long hard look at the resources you're giving to creativity. It's not just a question of the number of people you assign to the creative project: occasionally the number of participants can become a barrier, especially without a clear structure. The starting point is to look at the pool of people you have and see where you might need some more resource.

Ask yourself these questions: What time frame are we working to? If you're on a short-term project for a client, you may just need the equivalent of an SAS squad – small in number, tight on the process and able to deliver quickly with no frills. If it's a multi-stakeholder, long-term deal, you need an entirely different team and a rolling series of goals rather than a swift resolution. This may sound obvious, but the temptation to keep numbers low can lead to burnout in small teams. They're trying to do too much, with too few resources, and you risk your most valuable asset – your people.

Knowledge

Do you know enough about the end consumer? Do you have the information in-house so that you can analyze it to see what it tells you? Do you know what questions to ask that data? Or do you need another perspective? What are your competitors doing and doing well?

Ways of thinking/working

Who takes the ideas and makes them a plan? Is that responsibility with operations or logistics? Or both? In which case, should you add resource to help handle any tension that might happen as they work the idea into reality and delivery?

People

Have you a team of people who are curious, who like the notion of the new and who are willing to take on risks? If the answer is no, even the most highly motivated team may struggle. Even if only the core is curious, this will create momentum, plus other colleagues learn how the best ideas come to life.

Momentum

If you're doing something new, there will inevitably be setbacks. What is the motivation for keeping going? Do you need to add resources to those areas that can help keep the team going? It may be that at the start of your process the way you resource is different than when you're on your way or nearing completion. Don't be afraid to substitute people who can be benched for a while. As long as their contribution is recognized, and you are clear from the start that will be the approach, there should be no issues with running a tag team.

Occasionally it can be helpful to get a few new voices into the process. They have no axe to grind and they can be helpful in pointing out the small details that you have ignored given the intensity and focus on the idea in hand, or which you have simply not seen. Such as spelling the name of a key client incorrectly throughout a PowerPoint presentation. Luckily, that one got caught . . .

Take Action

Creativity can come from necessity and a pared-down team. This is not the only way, though. Instead try abundance. Double down on the problem, make resources available which can really deliver. Release people temporarily from other projects and see what happens if you create a bountiful team instead of working in the normal way.

Prompt the unconscious

The first season of *Columbo*, the iconic cop show based in LA, was aired in 1971. Over 50 years later it is still running on a TV channel somewhere near you, and is still popular. Starring Peter Falk, the show broke the mould of mystery dramas because you always learned whodunnit in the opening scenes. Frankly you also always know that the bumbling but brilliant blue-collar cop Columbo is going to catch them. But the intricate plotting, the twists and turns of how he identifies the villain, and his timeless catchphrase 'Just one more thing . . .' make the show compelling viewing. *Columbo* has stood the test of time, and became especially popular during the pandemic.

Its key ingredients are the brilliant acting, the routine underestimation of the detective by the perpetrator of the crime, and the exemplary attention to detail. Also classic are the running jokes, including Columbo's relationship with his adorable and lazy basset hound, called 'Dog', and his pride in his European car, an over-the-hill Peugeot 403 that is constantly being mistaken for scrap.

We love the show for all those reasons, *and* because it's educational. There is one brilliant episode that explains how powerful the unconscious can be, and how to exploit it. When you're problem-solving, or facing a challenging sell, it is really useful to understand this power and how to exploit it.

In the episode 'Double Exposure', which first aired in December 1973, the plot revolves around an ad executive who kills one of his clients who is threatening to whistle-blow about an extortion ring. The killer is an expert in motivational research and subliminal advertising. He inserts several single frames of cool drinks into the reels of a film – the frames go by too fast for the conscious mind to note them, but the mind picks them up subconsciously and makes the viewer crave what is pictured. At the same time he ensures his victim is eating salty snacks. When the man goes out to fetch a drink the crime takes place, and all the while the killer is alibied as he's narrating the film (he's pre-recorded the track, of course). Columbo learns about the expert's profession and eventually uses his own subliminal cuts to catch him.

From this TV drama we learn the power of the unconscious. And this is not fiction. In fact, subliminal advertising is so powerful that it has been banned in the United Kingdom, United States and Australia since the 1950s.

In the modern world of advertising there is a huge amount of work that goes into ensuring good attention for ads. There are more ads than ever, and there are more ways of avoiding them. Advertising has now become a battle for attention. *Forbes*, the business magazine, concludes: 'In the attention economy, every second counts. For brands, serving ad content that can hold a viewer's attention for longer not only leads to greater engagement, enhanced brand recall and improved trust with the consumer, it also positively affects their bottom line. Simply put, more attention means more sales.'

Except that there are two ways to process data and information. *High attention processing*, which relies on concentration; and *low attention processing*, which has more to do with how subliminal advertising works, and that episode of *Columbo*. Low attention processing lets the unconscious mind do the work. And the unconscious mind is actually more powerful.

This is the lizard part of your brain – the oldest part and the part concerned with the most important human impulse, survival. It is the part of the brain that is phylogenetically very primitive. Many people call it the *lizard brain*, because the limbic system is about all a lizard has for brain function. It is in charge of fight, flight, feeding, fear, freezing up and fornication. You can appeal to someone's lizard brain with implicit messaging rather than logic, and with emotional safety as a lead persuasion. We once saw a study which proved that for a company selling security doors the most successful images showed the doors ajar, not locked. Why? Because for children a shut door signals abandonment. Can you find the angle that will appeal to the lizard brain, the unconscious? We are not suggesting that you adopt disreputable means of persuasion. What you could do is consider the deep-rooted and emotional causes of the business challenge and take measures to do something about those. Or access neurolinguistic programming techniques such as mirroring your prospective customer, and framing your solution in visual, auditory and emotional ways. Reduce anxiety by tapping into childhood archetypes and delivering solutions that are more than transactional.

Take Action

If you can appeal to the unconscious mind when you're selling, persuading or leading a team, you are going to get further than logic alone will take you. Take a course in neurolinguistic programming (NLP). Help your team understand archetypes and use them to create.

Change direction

The story of the iconic Chuck Taylor All Star basketball shoe is a history of changing directions.

The Chuck Taylor All Star might be the most famous footwear ever. More than 60 per cent of Americans own or have owned a pair. Modern legends, from James Dean to Kurt Cobain, have worn them. Michelle Obama, Beyoncé, Rihanna, Katy Perry and Lady Gaga are all seen in them regularly – and the list goes on and on.

The company that originally produced the All Star was, in fact, a galoshes manufacturing business. Marquis Mills Converse opened the eponymous firm in 1908 in Massachusetts, to make winter rubber-soled footwear on a seasonal basis.

The first change of direction was in 1915. In order to keep the workforce employed all year round, the business began to produce sports shoes, which also made use of their core component part – rubber – to make the shoe waterproof, durable and more lightweight, with a grip better than leather.

In 1918 the Converse company made the first All Star shoe to supply the hugely popular sport of basketball. At first sales were limp. But thanks to another change of direction they soon skyrocketed, and this was due to one salesman.

Chuck Taylor played semi-professional basketball for the Akron Firestones in Ohio. In 1923, when he was still in his early twenties, he changed direction and became a salesman for Converse. He was so successful that in 1932 they added his name to the ankle patch on the shoe. He spent his life promoting basketball and the Chuck Taylor All Stars, travelling back and forth across the United States and living out of his car.

Then in 1957 came another pivot with the introduction of the Low Cut All Star, which became the hugely popular alternative for casual wear. Both styles are still massive today and sell worldwide. In the 1970s the Chuck Taylor All Star, once the footwear of choice for elite basketball players, became a countercultural shoe, and the owners began to produce them in myriad colours and styles. In the 1990s the company employed a Cool Hunter to spot next trends and promote their products with the coolest of marketing. The All Star is no longer used in the professional basketball game, but thanks to several changes of direction it has to qualify as one of the most successful and iconic sports shoes ever produced.

Here's another masterful pivot or change of direction. When we were children Lucozade, a popular UK-based energy drink, was marketed purely as a remedy for sick children. For decades there was a neon sign on the wall of the original factory in London, which could be seen from the Chiswick flyover and read: 'Lucozade aids recovery' – the strapline from the original TV ad.

The product was created by a pharmacist from Newcastle, William Walker Hunter, in 1927 from a mixture of glucose and fizzy water. In the 1970s, however, the relative health of the UK nation (fewer flu epidemics, and less sickness generally) meant that sales were in rapid decline.

In 1982 the brand changed direction, from a remedy for sick children to a sports drink. The strapline changed from 'aids recovery' to 'replaces lost energy'. The packaging changed from a large glass bottle wrapped in orange cellophane to a plastic single drink. The product stopped being sold in pharmacies and switched instead to supermarkets and local convenience stores and sweetshops. The new advertising campaign starred Daley Thompson, the hugely popular Olympic Gold medal-winning decathlete, and targeted everyday athletes instead of mums. All this changed the fortune of the brand, which has gone on to develop multiple formats and flavours.

Sometimes businesses need to change direction, finding new sources of growth in areas that are adjacent to historical strengths. Pivoting direction is a sign of creative strength. Sometimes people need to do this individually, too.

Since the 1980s, Sarah Kennedy has spent most of her career as a highly successful fashion journalist writing for the *Huffington Post*, *Telegraph*, Hearst magazines and the *New York Observer*. She's an author, of books including *Vintage Style: 25 Fashion Looks and How to Get Them* and *The Swimsuit: A Social History*.

After 40 years in journalism, and in her late 50s, she switched direction. In the charming (and for fans of the TV show *Gilmore Girls*, the familiar) Connecticut town of New Milford, Sarah has opened up a boutique selling vintage handbags, clothing and sustainably made housewares, health and beauty products: The Safari Collective. She started her change of direction with vintage handbags, which she hunted down in second-hand sales and then refurbished, teaching herself techniques from YouTube. Sarah has been searching for individual vintage style since she was a teenager. She told the *Independent* that her personal style dates from the late 1970s: 'I saw two ultra-cool girls in a club in Hull in 1979, who told me all their clothes were second-hand. I jettisoned my Disco Dolly look pretty darn quickly, went out the next day with five quid and bought a whole new wardrobe.'

Sarah says: 'It was a creative process, I wanted to do things with my hands. I was also tired of writing. I got to the point when I was at NY Fashion week in 2022. I thought, *I'm not doing this anymore. We're all writing the same thing; we're all scrambling around.* Fashion is full of middle-aged people who want it to stay the same. It's stifling, and exhausting. I decided I was done. I wanted to meet more people and stop sitting behind a computer.' She loves interacting with human beings everyday now (which writers don't always do).

Sarah points out that 'being creative isn't always about literally creating a painting or writing a book. Creativity is absolutely a state of mind, creativity and inspiration are linked.'

Sarah gave up a career with status. It was a big thing to turn her back on writing. But she was done. It was time to change direction. Sarah concludes, 'The older you get, the more important it is to look forward.'

Take Action

If you're stuck, if you're bored, or if your business is stalling, then change direction. How can you move to an adjacent path that will reap dividends for you? Remember, choices seem drastic when you are in the middle of making them, but if you take perspective, and elevate your point of view, you can see that a different direction might take you to a better place.

Make it iconic

We are surrounded by icons; we navigate our lives by their light.

In his book *How Brands Become Icons*, writer Douglas Holt says, 'The crux of iconicity is that the person or the thing is widely regarded as the most compelling symbol of a set of ideas or values that society deems important.' In the 1950s, James Dean or Harley motorcycles represented rebellion against the crushing mores of convention. Budweiser became the beer that championed overlooked ordinary men. In the 1980s, an advert for VW Golf became an iconic reflection of the independent woman.

Icons have mythology and a set of beliefs that draw people to them. As Holt adds: 'When you create a myth, consumers come to perceive the myth as embodied in the product. So they buy the product to consume the myth and to forge a relationship with the brand.'

Take your problem or challenge. It's time to bring in some spring light. Consider how it might become an icon and shine. What pressure in society can the issue represent an escape from? How can it represent the spirit that the zeitgeist needs?

Here are two examples from the world of advertising using techniques that build icons:

Hollywood-ify it – elevate the ordinary and put it on a pedestal
Make it eternal and give it scale

Hollywood-ify it

Some advertising puts the product on a pedestal. Sometimes elevating a simple everyday product with the most gorgeous of advertising is enough. Hovis brilliantly tapped into the power of nostalgia (remember the advert that showed a boy on a bicycle going up a hill with the strapline 'It's as good today as it's always been'?) and took a humble loaf from a commodity product to a taste of homecoming.

Make it eternal

Some brands deliver ruthlessly in terms of eternal iconicity. Celebration is nothing without Moët. Celebrating with a cup of tea is not the same. Never has been, and never will be. True eternal icons resist fundamental change. New York is an iconic city; it never changes but it continually reinvents.

There are some communications that elevate brand icons. Cinema is a medium that created stars and icons, and creative work shown in a cinema can deliver more desirability than the same work appearing in a social feed. It's possible to wonder at the premiums that glossy magazines demand for front section advertising, but the associations with supermodels and high fashion make the cost worth it. While TV retains its role as a channel for iconic advertising, everyone adores seeing their brand on an outstanding billboard – literally your name in lights.

Above all, be respectful. You can create icons, but icons can also fall. Think about how the brand can be iconic as a means to inject real creativity, but respect the icon that you create.

Take Action

What can you borrow from the world of icons to help solve a problem in the workplace? Icons can create a central belief or symbol that becomes a guiding light for the team or organization. This can be a new spring or a new dawn, bringing new light, green shoots and change. You can use iconic film stars, icons of past times, or iconic cultural events.

Give it purpose

During a visit to the NASA Space Centre in 1962, President Kennedy noticed a janitor carrying a broom. He interrupted his tour, walked over to him and said: 'Hi, I'm Jack Kennedy, what are you doing?' The janitor responded: 'I'm helping put a man on the moon, Mr President.'

Is everyone you work with clear about what they are doing there?

Often the job description, even the key performance indicators by which you will be judged, are not the real reason you are there. If the janitor at NASA was putting a man on the moon, not sweeping the floor, then what are *you* doing and how does it ladder up to the ultimate purpose of your organization? If you can ensure that everyone understands the purpose of the organization, you can unleash everyone's creativity to contribute to that purpose.

If the catering team in the office think they are only there to follow instructions and do things as cheaply as possible, you will get less creativity than if they know they're there to make your customers welcome (within a budget). And you'll have fewer mince pies or hot cross buns to celebrate the season. If the design team believe they are hired for efficiency, you will get less standout work than if they know your purpose.

Is the point of your job the same as the functions you perform? Unless you are a sole independent operator, the chances are that you are performing those functions as part of a team which has a bigger purpose. You should be very clear as to what that is. Making profits for the company you work for, soothing your immediate boss, or helping your clients to grow? If you're selling beds, is your purpose helping people to get a good night's sleep or to have more energy in the morning? If you're an accountant, are you making the books balance or really securing a viable future for the company and its employees?

The *Financial Times* wrote a report in February 2023 about *mattering*. Apparently, it's the new management buzzword coming your way from the lofty environs of Davos. Journalist Jemima Kelly (who is clearly irritated by this concept) writes: 'supposedly, the "secret to management in a new hybrid-working economy" is not honouring working hours, or making sure employees are achieving a proper work-life balance, or even just keeping in regular contact with them. No, the most crucial thing is "delivering and cultivating" something known as "mattering", the belief that you are important to others in your workplace.'

She goes on to say (unarguably): 'The way to make someone feel that they are valued is actually to value them'.

But mattering at work does go beyond feeling valued by co-workers, or a boss. It is about whether you know that what you do matters to the overall purpose of the organization.

Deloitte have published some new findings which substantiate the importance of ensuring that everything you do ladders up to the purpose of the organization.

From research of over 4000 employees they found that purpose really matters to employees, but that only half of those surveyed see their organization's purpose mirrored in their workplace reality. In fact, 47 per cent said they left for purpose-related reasons, and only 55 per cent see their leadership reflect the organization's purpose. There is a clear competitive advantage to be driven here, in terms of retaining and attracting talent by reducing what Deloitte call *the purpose gap*.

Barclays, one of the UK's biggest high street banks, asked their staff to become 'Digital Eagles' to customers. This began as a grassroots programme in 2013, which then became a promotional advertising campaign for the brand and a key pillar in restoring customer trust in the brand. The Digital Eagles team, which started as an enthusiastic bunch of just 12 employees, grew into a team of thousands who reached out to those customers lacking digital skills. Clearly this was in the best interests of the bank, who were relying on customers converting to online and app banking. The more widespread digital confidence was, the better the chance of this strategy succeeding. However, it didn't just have commercial outcomes. The scheme helped to alleviate customer anxiety (in the UK four out of five people admit to losing sleep over money worries). It gave the staff satisfaction and purpose. And it extended into care homes, where it played a role in helping people stay in touch during lockdown with loved ones. The Digital Eagles continue to help customers today, and specialize in helping them spot fraud online. All this builds confidence in the brand and gives purpose to the employees – 9 out of 10 stated that their work gives them a sense of personal achievement.

In a high-functioning team everyone knows their immediate and their ultimate purpose. It's great to be appreciated for what you do, and it is even better to know that what you do matters.

Take Action

Ensure that you are clear about the big purpose of your activity. And that everyone in the organization understands what this is and how to contribute. By unleashing your full team's energy towards the ultimate purpose, you'll get the best and most creative ideas every day. Check in with the people you work with, and gently ask them what they think they are there to deliver. If they don't fully get the purpose, you should workshop with them to co-create their own clarity around what they are really there for.

Random link

This is a great technique for when you are really stuck – stuck in the mud. Desperate for some green shoots to grow, like in early March when you are buffeted by the winds and rains of departing winter. When you are really stuck, pick an object – any object – and make a random link.

We first came across this technique in training from ?What If!. ?What If! are a creativity incubator for business and are now part of Accenture. We came across them in the early 2000s when they were an independent. They were set up in 1992 to help businesses run innovation projects, and their mantra is: 'Behave creatively and you will feel creative'.

The *random link technique* has two rules:

The random item must be truly random. If it has any kind of connection with what you're working on, then it doesn't work.

You must keep working to find a connection, however improbable.

Let's do one right now.

How best can we explain the random link technique?

Reaching into our pocket, we find a scrunched-up tissue. Probably been there since the last time we wore this outfit. What is the connection between a used tissue and a business problem?

Tissues revolutionized women's lives. Both of our mothers were home keepers and caregivers. As part of their weekly routines they washed, and ironed, large white handkerchiefs for their husbands. In the 1950s and early 1960s, this was the norm. A man carried a white handkerchief, to wipe the sweat from his brow, and to offer to any lady who might meet it. Women also carried handkerchiefs, which they gifted to each other (they were the scented candle of their day), and which also needed washing and ironing. However, ladies carried smaller, embroidered items. In our experience, if you had any kind of runny nose, you needed a dad's handkerchief to be of any use. The whole thing was sexist, and typical of attitudes prevailing at the time.

Tissues had been around since 1924, but in the mid-1950s Kleenex began an ad campaign that stated: 'Don't put a cold in your pocket . . . use once and destroy, germs and all.' When the revolutionary fashion trends of the 1960s meant that men stopped wearing traditional suits with a featured handkerchief pocket, the days of the handkerchief were numbered, and by the 1980s they were rare.

Our mums were delighted. Who wants to wash germ-ridden items and iron linen if they don't have to? Now, however, younger generations, passionate about sustainability, are questioning single-use items. Despite the pandemic, might we see a trend back to the handkerchief? *Wired* magazine editor Adrienne So thinks we might, writing: 'Sustainability is a big issue around here, and if you've already replaced your paper towels with bamboo ones, it's time to give the hankie some consideration. But beyond practicality and sustainability, a hankie gives me pleasure in a way that a tissue never could.'

With the tissue as a random link, we can think of at least four connections possible for a business problem.

First random link connection: The tissue took a chore away from the home keeper. Is there a way of cutting an unnecessary chore out of the working process? Are there any parts of it that are as tedious and as unnecessary as ironing a square of linen for a man to put into his suit pocket?

Second random link connection: Now younger people are questioning the ethics of a single-use item. Is there a more sustainable way of managing the process? Are there any single-use items that can be eliminated by adding in a reusable product?

Third random link connection: It was usual for men to carry a big handkerchief and women to carry a smaller item. Is the product designed for one-size-fits-all? It could be that you need more specific sizes, either by gender or simply height and weight. *Invisible Women: Exposing Data Bias in a World Designed for Men*, by Caroline Criado Perez, is a fantastic book that points out the real dangers present in everyday items like seat belts, designed to keep men safe, not people. Alternatively, could one product spec serve everyone? Is there wastage? Or might you speak to more people if you tailor the look and feel to more cohorts of people?

Fourth random link connection: The used tissue had hung around in our pocket and we had failed to throw it away despite it having served its purpose and being contaminated with germs. How can you ensure that waste items are disposed of in a timely fashion, and can this help efficiencies or hygiene in the workplace? We left a used tissue in a pocket, to our shame. It is doing us no good at all, other than to provide a random link for this example.

Take Action

If you're stuck, pick a random object and find a link to your problem. As you can see, literally anything will do. Find a small team, pick a random object, and keep a note of where it takes you and what ideas come from the exercise.

Spring forward and be more *dog*

What on earth does that mean? Is one of the first responses to the idea that being more *dog* might make you more creative. When did animal behaviour ever become one of the notions behind how we might work? Although many of us may sometimes feel like swans at work – all seeming calm on the surface while our desperate underwater efforts remain concealed – dogs are not a normal work metaphor.

However, when we explore this idea a little further, there is a lot to be learned from dogs. Dogs are naturally curious, always wanting to explore, and as any dog owner will tell you, the walk you do every day is still full of exploration and excitement for dogs, no matter how many times they have walked those same streets, woods or beaches. Could being more *dog* help us be more creative in what might seem like a usual way of working or pattern of approach? It's a bit like when you start a new role – yes, you may have done the same thing, but it was somewhere else. What's new and or even a little bit different to where you were before? Or are there big differences, which you can both learn from and use to launch new ideas? The dread phrase *We've always done it this way* should act as a warning – isn't there even a slight change you could make? The tendency with doing it the same way, always, is that it becomes habit. And habit isn't a great basis for creativity to flourish.

Being more *dog* also means being eager and enthusiastic. When we're trying to develop new ideas, one of the tendencies is to stress-test the idea. To break it down into its component parts, to encourage people to find any faults or issues. This has a role – of course it does – but how about being *more dog*?

Being more *dog* means playing with your idea, seeing how big you could make it if you wanted to. In being more playful, we let creativity, rather than cold hard logic, take centre stage.

So how do we achieve this state?

Firstly, let yourself and your colleagues come into the situation as if you were new to the issue that you want to change. The walk-through that you're about to take might be familiar, but how about looking for new elements that habits or process might have ignored? What could be new in a method or way of working? Do the same people always work together? Do they always do the same aspects of the task or approach? Why not ask them to swap roles? Get the new occupant of the role to write down three or more new things that they think could create change. Any more than three, and you run the risk of diluting the creativity of the new approach, and may just get a long list of random ideas which aren't the best that the team can create and deliver. Three ideas are actionable, a small novel isn't.

Take Action

Lose the cynicism, lose the ennui. Give all your enthusiasm to this project and the team. Don't think about the consequences in the long term. For now, suspend any disbelief and charge forwards. What is the most fun you can have with this? Chase that ball, with all of the excitement of a puppy.

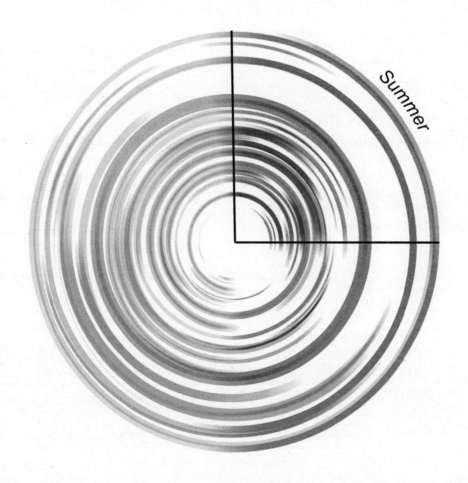

Summer

CHAPTER FOUR

Summer – how organizations can flower and be fruitful

Summer creativity practices are fundamental yet also joyful.

Let's start with one business whose fortunes were revolutionized because the Director of Operations and Marketing went on a trip to Europe.

In 1982 Howard Schultz quit a well-paying job in New York and joined Starbucks, which at the time had five Seattle stores. In 1983 he went on a business trip to Italy, and experienced the charms of Italian coffee bars in Milan and Verona. He returned to America determined to recreate the distinctive Italian espresso bar experience there. But the store owners were unconvinced. Schultz returned, full of ideas of a relaxed third place between home and work, where good coffee was served and there were no demands to drink up and move along. He found himself captivated by the sense of community he had found in the city's espresso bars – the moments of human connection. But he failed to convince his bosses. And so Schultz left, convinced that his gut instincts were right, even if he couldn't persuade the then owners of Starbucks that departing from their relatively successful existing business template would lead to growth. Determined to make his vision real, he returned to Italy and visited over 500 coffee bars. He then went out to raise funds for his own business. He approached over 240 investors – and 217 rejected his ideas. His persistence, based on an emotional experience and backed up by research, is remarkable. Eventually he raised the cash to open his own store,

Il Giornale. In 1988 the original Starbucks management sold their stores to Schultz, who rebranded his coffeehouses as Starbucks and began an expansion programme that changed the way people lived, worked and socialized.

Of course, we know the rest of the story. When we were growing up in the UK, there were two options if you wanted a drink. There were cafés that sold sandwiches, full English breakfasts (bacon, eggs, black pudding and toast), instant coffee and builder's tea. They weren't that welcoming, and they certainly didn't allow you to stay after you had finished your drinks and meal. And then there were pubs. If you wanted to linger over a drink, your only option was the pub – during opening hours, and when you were over 18. Starbucks revolutionized the high street, giving teens a safe and welcoming place to meet and socialize, and providing a transformed experience of sitting on your own as a woman – pubs were never that welcoming of sole women customers, and when we were in our early twenties, they'd laugh (at best) at anyone ordering a non-alcoholic drink, and they didn't serve coffee or tea. Seats in cafés and pubs were at hard tables with hard-backed chairs.

The prologue to Schultz's account of the Starbucks story, *Pour Your Heart Into It: How Starbucks Built a Company One Cup at a Time*, reads as follows: 'Care more than others think wise; Risk more than others think safe; Dream more than others think practical; Expect more than others think possible.' Schultz states that Starbucks is 'living proof that a company can lead with its heart and nurture its soul and still make money'. If that sounds romantic, it is.

Starbucks can polarize people. Some people resent the homogeneity of the stores, the very American-ness of the experience, and reject its marketing as gimmickry. Whatever your response, however, it is impossible to deny its success, and the way in which it changed how people spend their disposable income, and indeed their disposable time. When Starbucks introduced sofas into their 'third space' cafés, it took people by surprise. Today the idea that you can linger, write your novel or work outside the office is taken for granted. The human connection created between baristas and customers when they ask for your name to put on your order is still charming; even if it has sometimes become subject to humour, it is still very personal. To think that this comes down to one man's vision, his stubborn conviction, and his summer trip to Italy is inspiring. Schultz says:

> There are moments in our lives when we summon the courage to make choices that go against reason, against common sense, and the wise counsel of people we trust. But we lean forward nonetheless because despite all risks and rational argument we believe that the path we are choosing is the right and best thing to do. We refuse to be bystanders, even if we do not know exactly where our actions will lead . . . Belief in what is right catapults us over hurdles.

Sometimes at work it is time to follow protocol, to keep within the guidelines, to fill out the spreadsheets, to tick the right boxes, to colour only between the lines and to maintain maximum efficiency over leaps into the unknown.

Sometimes, though, it is time to follow your dreams, act on gut instinct and take a plunge into the unknown and unaccountable. Here are 13 creative techniques to facilitate your path and progress.

Indulge your gut instinct
Re-express with different language
Be more *pirate*
Be bored
Give into your worst impulse
What won't you do? And why?
Do nothing
Use an old idea
Work against your better judgement

Build back better
What would someone else say?
Take a trip
Be more *Wimbledon*

Indulge your gut instinct

There's a lot of science behind gut instinct these days, thanks to Nobel prize winner Daniel Kahneman. He got his award for work on what he called *System 1* and *System 2 thinking*. System 2 is your conscious brain, the part of you that makes rational decisions based on evidence. System 1, the predominant bit in most unconscious decisions (and according to Kahneman nearly all decisions), is your gut instinct, your emotionality, your deep-rooted biases and preconceptions.

Kahneman's international bestselling book outlining his ideas, *Thinking Fast and Slow*, challenged the idea that economics worked on the basis of humans being rational. He showed instead that economics really operates on the basis of dumb instinct.

When we saw Kahneman speak at a conference, he said: 'People think that they are the Oval Office (i.e. logical and considered). In fact they are the Press Office (wildly responding to emotion).' Kahneman definitively shows that we think we make decisions on a rational basis, but in fact we usually don't. We make them on the basis of powerful instincts that have evolved over millennia.

In his book *Blink: The Power of Thinking Without Thinking*, New York writer Malcolm Gladwell argues that in all of our brains, there is a mighty backstage process, which works its will subconsciously. 'Through this process we have the capacity to sift huge amounts of information, blend data, isolate telling details and come to astonishingly rapid conclusions, even in the first two seconds of seeing something.'

If you have ever been looking for a new place to live, you have probably experienced this. Whatever the rational reasons for choosing a property to rent or to buy, you really make your mind up in those first 30 seconds when you walk through the door.

Blink contains the story of the psychologist John Gottman, who since the 1980s has worked with more than 3000 married couples in a small room, his 'love lab', near the University of Washington. He videotapes them having a conversation. Reviewing just an hour's worth of each tape, Gottman has been able to predict with 95 per cent accuracy whether that couple will be married 15 years later. If he watches only 15 minutes of tape, his success rate is about 90 per cent. Scientists in his lab have determined they can usually predict whether a marriage will work after watching just three minutes of conversation between newly-weds. Gladwell calls this ability *thin-slicing* – finding patterns based on little experience – and argues that we all do it all the time.

The arguments about gut instinct don't originate with Kahneman or Gladwell. Plato, writing around 370 BCE, described human nature as a charioteer in charge of two horses. One is human and ignoble, the other is sublime and winged.

And the *Katha Upanishad* (dated from the 5th to 1st century BCE) tells us: 'Know the Self as Lord of the chariot, the body as the chariot itself, the discriminating intellect as the charioteer, and the mind as the reins. The senses, say the wise, are the horses; selfish desires are the roads they travel.'

So, everyone agrees, we all operate at some level on gut instinct deep down. The question is: *How should you deploy this in business, when your organization prides itself on rational data-driven decisions?*

Instinct or algorithm? It's a question that Karen Blackett OBE asked her three interviewees at her Chancellor's Dinner at Portsmouth University in 2019.

Kanya King OBE, supercool founder of the MOBO Organisation, said instinct. Sir Lenny Henry CBE, fresh from raising money for Comic Relief, said instinct too. But Tom Ilube OBE, tech entrepreneur, chose the algorithm (as you might predict, using your instincts).

Every time we jump in the car, the same question comes up. Should we turn on Waze? Should we use our instincts? Surely Waze's algorithm knows more than we do, and so it proves – until there's an unexpected road closure and you wind up with us and everyone else trapped in Wazelocked traffic.

Lenny Henry talked about the big break he got from Chris Tarrant. When Lenny was new to *Tiswas*, the weekend kids' TV show, Tarrant took him for lunch and told him he was failing to make the transition to presenter from stand-up and would soon be off the show. He suggested that Lenny pivot and try a different approach. Lenny listened, followed his advice and soon this turned him into a star. Karen asked him why he thought that Chris Tarrant had bothered to stage this intervention. Lenny said: 'He saw the potential in me.' Tarrant saw something even when Lenny was screwing up, and he trusted his instincts. Don't trust that any algorithm could have delivered on that potential fame, and a career that aside from the laughter has helped raise over £1 billion for Comic Relief.

A black box thrown into a tech stack can certainly do a lot of automated heavy lifting, but there is still a need for human intervention to guide what the algorithms are trying to achieve as well as to augment their outputs. Delegating this responsibility to an opaque black box to make **all** the decisions is short-sighted – as the algorithm is only a part of the process. It cannot define what data to assess, how that data should be featured and how to interpret the results in line with commercial goals.

'All my best decisions are made with heart, guts and taste.' This quote is from Jeff Bezos, a man who has revolutionized business with data. Use the data but trust your heart.

Take Action

Review the data, listen to the logic, ask a generative AI site like ChatGPT what its (logical) answer would be, and then, instead, trust your heart and your gut instinct.

Re-express with a different language

One of the frustrations of the workplace can be the feeling that you are talking but that no one is listening. Or that they *are* listening but not doing what you wanted them to really listen to. Perhaps people are listening to you but not hearing you. You feel that you have spoken clearly and concisely and then everyone goes off and does what you see as the wrong things, in the wrong order, at the wrong time.

Whatever the situation, it needs to be addressed, particularly if we're going to create a sense of the new. If you are the person leading the project, it's important to remember that while you may have been immersed in the issues around new product development for weeks, it's probable that your crack team of creative thinkers hasn't. So, you start to talk about the issues and all they hear is a litany of barriers in their way, rather than an opportunity.

Starting off by saying: *This really is an important task and if we don't crack it, the company is at risk* might appeal to the daredevil attitude of some team members. Others may think it's time to start looking for another role if they're going to keep making their rent. It also places them under huge pressure, and pressure is not conducive to creativity. Set your scene by changing the language – it's about an opportunity to change the future of the company, rather than a do-or-die brainstorm to avoid corporate oblivion.

It's also important to explain what the *Why* is. Why are you doing this? Why were those people chosen? This is a great chance to recognize the talents of the individual members of your team and to validate them. In their *Harvard Business Review* article '4 Reasons Employees Lose their Motivation', Richard E. Clark and Bror Saxberg discuss *values mismatch* as one of the reasons why colleagues lose motivation. Values mismatch is when a colleague isn't connected to the value of the task, so they feel disinclined to do it. This can be particularly relevant on creative elements of work, because these may not be seen as core to their job role. We've discussed elsewhere about why people don't identify as creative, and those limiting perceptions can get in the way of the work at hand. Your language should demonstrate that you understand those concerns and that what they are doing will make a difference.

In changing your language, it's key to bring some passion to the scene setting and the task ahead. *I'm excited by this opportunity* works far better than *The board asked me to pull this team together*.

Re-expressing yourself can also help frame the task in a different light, one that looks full of possibilities. It's unlikely that the creators of video-sharing platforms saw their role in society as enabling the global obsession with cat videos, but it's happened as a by-product of a bigger scenario.

Is it worth thinking about your task in a different way and expressing it in light of that thinking?

We're trying to make this a better experience for consumers, so they have more time to enjoy their lives outside of work may motivate people more than the idea of thinking for six weeks about a work calendar tool that reduces the need to input certain information repeatedly.

It's also worth expressing your issue in the language of your end user. No real person has ever talked about optimizing the CRM database as a way to really personalize communication, but real people do get annoyed when they get emails that don't recognize who they are. Asking if you want to opt out of Mother's Day emails is an elegant way to recognize that your customers may not be part of that occasion. Get the language right and communication can really flow. If the language really changes, you get communication and conversation, which is where ideas start to thrive.

Take Action

Re-express with different words. Simply replacing key words in your creative challenge will enable your team to think differently. If your challenge is keeping clients, then use a metaphor like marriage counselling, or renewing deep trust. Or you could re-express from a different perspective – instead of asking: *How do we keep clients*, ask: *Why would a client stay loyal to us?*

Be more *pirate*

There is a brilliant book on this by Adam Morgan, *The Pirate Inside: building a challenger within yourself and your organization.*

Adam Morgan advises businesses on how to challenge bigger and more established rivals. Morgan's book on pirates came about because he found that it was one thing to come up with ideas for differentiation and challenge, another to follow through on them in an organization that was built for preserving the status quo.

Why pirates? Morgan writes that the Navy follows the rules, and pirates break them. In a world where the only guarantee is continuous change, it helps to break the rules before a challenger breaks them and gains advantage.

How can this work for you?

First of all, in any situation it is good to establish what the Navy is, and what it believes. If there is a firm hierarchy in your organization, what about creating a Gen Z board to come up with ideas from their grass roots position? (Gen Z is the name used to refer to the generation born between 1996 and 2010, who grew up with the climate crisis, COVID, economic downturn and gender fluidity, and with their lives often lived on social media.) In our previous book, *Belonging*, we found striking differences in attitudes to work among people under 25. Our research for the book (conducted by Dynata in February 2020 and August 2021) showed that in many respects the norms of a conventional workplace are unacceptable to younger people. Take banter – one in three people overall find it uncomfortable, but this rises to half of people under 25. One in three people have either witnessed, or experienced bias, harassment or inappropriate behaviour at work. Again this rises to half of the under 25s. Of course, harassment should be unacceptable to everyone, but it might be that most older people at work put up with unacceptable behaviour simply because they've had to put up with it their whole working lives. Gen Z, on the other hand, will not. And in many other respects this age group have different values, shaped by the unprecedented events of the early 2020s. If you have a segment of the workforce in this age group, give them access to senior management by creating a Gen Z board. They can give you feedback about the culture and you can ask them for ideas that are influencing them. This is definitely an intervention that is anti-Navy and more *pirate*.

One of the other key things about those real-life pirates was the Pirate Articles. Going to sea in the golden age of pirates was a high-risk venture. People were leaving home for an unspecified and extremely hazardous time. The Pirate Articles represented a set of mutual agreements for their adventure. They included a promise that no one would abandon the enterprise until it had reaped rewards. That all profits would be shared. That all arguments were suspended until the crew were back on land. Can you create a Pirate constitution for the team you are working with in this way? It will have two brilliant outcomes if you can. First everyone understands that they are a team and can have different points of view about what is next but that these disagreements must get aired and resolved. Second, that everyone is committed to each other and to mutual success and triumph. The ship doesn't go back to harbour until you have succeeded.

One more key thing about pirates was the diversity of the crew. Long John Silver is one of the most famous pirates in literature (from *Treasure Island* by Robert Louis Stevenson) and he had of course a missing leg. Captain Hook from *Peter Pan* had a missing hand. They didn't let that stop them bossing the crew or from being fantastically entertaining. At a time when it is still very unusual for disabled people to run organizations, pirates were proof that the reluctance in business to this day to entrust leadership in this way is both unfair and excluding. There were many women pirates, fighting alongside and equally with the men on ship. Anne Bonny and Mary Read sailed in Calico Jack's crew and were said to fight with more skill than any man on board. Grace O'Malley forged a career in piracy from the age of 11 and was considered a fierce leader at sea and a shrewd politician who successfully petitioned Queen Elizabeth I to release her imprisoned relatives. It's said that she fought off an ambush within one hour of giving birth.

What is the make-up of your team? Do you all look similar, and come from similar backgrounds? Be more *pirate* and ensure that you have a bunch of glorious misfits thinking imaginatively and outside of the norm and status quo with you.

Take Action

Be more pirate. Start with a team commitment to the cause, lose any hierarchy and make sure that your circle is full of wonderful misfits.

Be bored

We're not sure how it works for you, but going on a fly-and-flop holiday can be really productive. You go back to work rested, relaxed and quite often with some new thoughts around work. The key thing is to remember that great insight you had before you tucked into your delicious spaghetti vongole. Oh, and your passport; remember that too . . .

We all remember those long, long summer afternoons, where it's just easier to sit and do nothing. This is where you are letting creativity be unproductive, which sounds counter to the purpose of the book but which can actually be a great tactic. When we're searching for inspiration or a new way of thinking, it's often the case that we become quite desperate as we search for *the* answer. We're so eager to get to an answer, any answer sometimes, that we force the process and accept any result that seems possible. That's not creativity, it's a method of finding the lowest common denominator which appears to address your problem. If creativity were that easy, we'd all be creative, all the time, and you wouldn't be reading this book.

By being lazy and perhaps borderline bored, you are encouraging your subconscious to allow the problem to bubble through your mind. By taking your conscious mind out of the loop (even though it's always on), you are finding a way for yourself to make non-linear links between the various elements of the issue that you face. It's interesting that something as everyday as a long bath or a long shower can give you the opportunity to let your thoughts expand. It's said that the writer Aaron Sorkin (of *The West Wing* fame and winner of multiple awards – an Oscar and BAFTA and several Golden Globes and Emmys) could always resolve a tricky plot line by having a long shower. The story is that to encourage his creativity, a shower was installed next to his office so that when needed, he could drum up some creativity while under the water. Clean and creative, what a combination!

As we are not suggesting a plumbing revolution in the workplace layout, what else can you find to let your hours be boring but blessed with a solution? One way is to find an experience that isn't adjacent to the problem you're facing, but which could give you knowledge that could help unlock the solution. Do we think that Formula One and surgery have much in common, for example? Interestingly, the two have come together to find better ways of working. By using the simulation technology, data management and predictive analysis of Formula One, over one hundred surgeons got feedback on improving their technique. A sensor placed on a surgeon's arm sent information via Bluetooth to produce a data stream on their way of working, giving full feedback on technique and ways to improve. It's not a natural link, but in allowing that knowledge and experience to filter through, unexpected connections can happen. Using the same tools that calculate whether to take a pit stop, or to hang on a few more laps before you change tyres and so gain a place advantage, might not seem like a natural way of improving surgery, but it has had life-changing effects. The other key element of this was that it was feedback given without emotion or bias – it was just your work, analysed and with no human filter. As we know, we are afraid to be told our ideas or performance aren't great, but in this situation, the focus was improvement, impassively delivered and without any emotion.

By embracing a less forced approach, we give ourselves space to think. Or rather, not think but just let ideas develop and gain strength. By allowing ourselves and our teams to feel that we and they have the space to develop, we're giving ourselves permission to think about anything that could lead to a solution.

Assuming that we're not all going on holiday en masse, how do we bring those boring moments into your everyday workplace? Some organizations have encouraged teams to plan treasure hunts as a way of developing both team collaboration and a way of encouraging problem-solving. If you're doing this, please ensure that those people setting the problems aren't the only ones who ever get to the answer – we're trying to build teams and thinking here, not win a contest over obscure knowledge. If you're doing this type of activity, don't force it but allow colleagues to walk, and talk, and experience new ways of working.

Take Action

Plan some downtime for you to work things through, or for the team to relax away from problems. Often the team bonding event comes at the end of an awayday. Kick off with some meaningless activity instead, and create the conditions for inspiration.

Give into your worst impulse

What is that exactly?

According to Robert Bly, the poet and activist, we all drag a (metaphorical) long bag behind us through life. From the moment our parents or caregivers first say to us: 'Can't you sit still?' or 'It isn't nice to hit your brother', we take the bits of us our parents don't approve of and put them in the bag. Then we get to school where we hear: 'Good children don't get angry over such little things.' So we take our anger and we put it in that bag. That bag is full of our worst impulses. As we get older, we often put spontaneity in that bag. Bly warns that the more we shove in the bag, the more likely it is to burst.

If we look at toddlers' impulses, we can see a very clear theme. In the scout hut in Friern Barnet in North London, which also serves as a martial arts venue and a toddler daycare, there is a battered sign that reads: 'Toddlers' Rules'.

There are 10 of these:

1. If I like it, it's mine.
2. If it's in my hand, it's mine.
3. If I can take it from you, it's mine.
4. If I had it a little while ago, it's mine.
5. If it's mine, it must NEVER appear to be yours in any way.
6. If I'm doing or building something, all the pieces are mine.
7. If it looks just like mine, it is mine.
8. If I saw it first, it's mine.
9. If you are playing with something and you put it down, it automatically becomes mine.
10. If it's broken, it's yours.

So, worst instinct number 1: Make it yours.

You might have repressed this instinct. Indeed, if you are a functioning adult in a team you definitely have. This creative technique, though, relies on you going back to that instinct of ownership, even to the point of stealing. Remember that maxim often ascribed to Picasso: 'Good artists copy. Great artists steal.'

If you are stuck with a problem at work which needs a creative solution, can you borrow one and apply it to your situation? It is a common business practice after all. Supermarkets make own label replicas of famous brands and sell them at a cheaper price. When tech companies are challenged by start-ups, their first instinct is either to buy the company (Meta bought WhatsApp), or to try and duplicate the idea. A pioneer in the market can lead to many thriving copies. Starbucks was the first coffee shop brand to offer sofas and then free Wi-Fi. Now you can't move for similar venues on many high streets and shopping centres in towns and cities around the world.

Do give in to that toddler instinct, look around for the best possible answer and make it yours.

Worst instinct number 2: inertia.

Maybe you just have run out of steam and can't be bothered any more. Perhaps creativity feels like too much effort. You're not even halfway through the ideas in this book, but the energy required to be sparky has just run out.

Go with that instinct. Do nothing. Wait.

Wait by Frank Partnoy praises the Useful Art of Procrastination. It explains why we like to make snap decisions, and how to snap out of it. It is all about the capacity to look at situations with some long-term perspective. Behavioural economists have found a way of calculating this. The *discount rate* is the amount we are prepared to pay to wait. You will have heard of the experiment with the toddlers where they are offered one marshmallow now, or two in a few minutes. Experiments show that for long-term prosperity those toddlers that can bear to wait have better chances. This *discount rate* changes, however, over time. For example, if you are offered the choice of £50 today by your boss, or £100 in a month – which would you choose? Many people, for all kinds of rational and emotional reasons, would take the £50 today (while the offer is definitely good!). But if your boss offered you £50 in a year, or £100 in 13 months, which would you take? I bet you said you'd wait for the £100. The wait is the same – it's still one month's delay. But loads more people will opt to wait for another month with a year's perspective.

Delay any actions, and while you're doing this your unconscious mind might find you the new and creative answer.

Take Action

What is your worst instinct in this situation? For a while, just for a while, give into it and see what happens.

What won't you do? And why?

Most people are familiar with the idea of self-limiting beliefs. You don't know where they come from, but they act as very strong psychological brakes on what you do. They prevent you from pushing yourself into risky areas and they manifest as a nagging voice in your head which you can't keep quiet. Isn't it strange that companies, made up of all types of people, can create their own self-limiting beliefs that come to define their future? Do you think your organization has a mindset that minimizes your potential? Where does it come from? Is it overt or covert? Is it cultural, organizational or driven by management attitude that causes it? And most importantly, how can you change it so you can be better?

Of course, there can be other factors that determine what you do. You may be assessing your supplier list as you aim to become more sustainable. You may seek to support businesses owned by underrepresented groups as a key element of your Inclusion and Belonging plan. All of those decisions are part of a wider company drive towards a long-term and ethics-driven stance.

Sometimes, however, your actions may be determined by another series of factors. History can be one of them. Your company tried to do something new in a particular area and it didn't work, so you have never bothered to try again. It may not occur to the team that your customer base or your team capability has changed.

You could be a smaller, challenger brand that thinks that you will never be able to supplant a more dominant competitor, so you build incrementally.

It could be that your company culture doesn't use failing as a way of learning, so all your plans are safe, with predictable outcomes. Obviously, no company plans to fail, even though from an outside perspective it was obvious that they would.

So, what won't you do and why?

Will you cannibalize an existing product to facilitate the development of a new one?

Will you drop a long-held idea or concept?

Will you break up existing structures to help develop new ways of working?

What are you willing to risk to be inventive and creative? Team cohesion? A workstream?

Are you ready to work in an entirely different way, with little backup and a lot of commitment before you get a result? Or are you slow and steady in your outlook?

You have to ask yourself these questions before you come up with an idea because pulling back when you hit those hard edges can be difficult.

You also need to establish the ground rules for your change process. Is it going to be the same team all the way through or are you going to run a squad system? In your squad system, team members are rotated depending on need or contribution or capacity. You can and must apply the squad system to the leadership too, if that's required. Sarah may be brilliant at goal setting and inventiveness, but perhaps we need Janet to come in when we get to the delivery part. Are you willing to do that and can you explain that to everyone involved? They will need to buy in too.

Your goal setting and plans must recognize and respect what your boundaries are. You must also be willing to explain why those boundaries exist to your creative pioneers. In articulating why they exist, you might find a way of defining them as an opportunity, rather than a limit. So, what will you do, and how and who is going with you?

Take Action

Run an exercise to establish the limits, the things that you really will not do. Find the boundaries, then challenge them. Why are they the boundaries? Is it outdated thinking, conventional wisdom or common sense? Breaking them might be an opportunity to break the mould and gain advantage.

Do nothing

What are the consequences of doing nothing?

We live in an always on, full-throttle world that never seems to stop. Ask people how they are and they nearly always say: 'Busy!' with a rueful shrug and a half smile. It is almost as if we prove to ourselves and others just how essential we are by doing tasks continually and filling our days with to-do lists and what's next.

So, it's interesting to read in *Idleness: A Philosophical Essay* by Brian O'Connor, professor of philosophy at University College, Dublin, who argues that in being hyper-busy, we're stifling ourselves and our output. The deep satisfaction of incorporating doing nothing into your life has mental and health benefits. In doing nothing, you can lower your blood pressure, relax your skeletal muscles and sharpen your focus. All this can be achieved – just by doing nothing. However, it seems that as a society we find doing nothing quite alien and don't quite know how to deal with it. Take, for example, the study that took place at the University of Virginia, which recruited hundreds of undergraduate students and community members and asked them to take part in an experiment on 'thinking periods'. Volunteers were placed in a minimally furnished room, without their telephones or even a pen and paper, and were asked just to think. No distractions at all. There were two tests of between 6 and 15 minutes and students were either left to think or prompted to think about a subject – their next holiday, or a sport they were interested in, for example. Fifty per cent of the sample didn't like the experiment at all. So the location of the experiment was moved to the participants' homes, to see if that would improve the results. It didn't – it seems we don't like being left alone with our thoughts. In fact, we are so uncomfortable that when the students were asked to participate again, this time in a laboratory, an even more surprising thing happened. Rather than be left to think, 67 per cent of men and 25 per cent of the women taking part chose to give themselves an electric shock rather than be left just to think.

How is it that we find ourselves so uncomfortable with being left with our thoughts? It might be that we feel guilty that we're not ticking off our to-do list or being visibly active in our roles. Or we could just be concerned about where our minds will take us and how we deal with that lack of control. How many people do you know who gave up on mindfulness because practising it for 10 minutes a day became yet another thing to feel guilty about or because they spent the 10 minutes not being mindful, but being stressed about not being mindful enough? By not doing anything, will anything get done?

There is evidence that not doing anything *does* do something. When we sit and be, without constant cognitive engagement, we go into the default mode network (DMN) in our minds. It's where we go sometimes in conversations when we wander off and have to drag ourselves back to listen to what's being said. In DMN, our minds wander and link the dots and dashes in our minds together in a new way; we reset what we are thinking and we make leaps of connections and creativity.

The other side of not doing anything at a corporate level is that you may not need to do anything right now. It could be that just coasting along for a while will allow a new opportunity to open up that you couldn't force into being. The chance to absorb where you are now, without having a set path or plan, could be the corporate DMN you need to come back with new concepts and ideas or products. The corporate hive mind may be all the better for a break, and so too the organization.

Take Action

In fact, don't. Do nothing. Literally. It will be interesting to see what the consequences are of this. It might be that after a period of nothingness, new ideas come to you.

Use an old idea

The world of communications is all digital now, right? Where 50 years ago we had to go to a library to research things, now we simply search on our smartphones, and the rise of generative AI and large language learning models has transformed research in ways unimagined when your authors were at university in the 1980s.

Writing a letter is a charming anachronism now, and choosing to communicate by sending mail is complicated by the cost in terms of the calculation of carbon footprints.

However, one old idea has proved commercially surprisingly successful.

Unsolicited direct mail in paper form has had a revival in fortunes.

It's especially true that digital natives (people who don't remember the world before the internet) welcome direct mail. Those aged 15–24 are most likely to trust direct mail (out of everyone surveyed in a recent report). For people who are accustomed to interacting digitally, a physical invitation to buy proves both novel and effective. And in terms of carbon footprint, the right message delivered in the right way can be better than digital bombardment.

There is much to be said too for recycling old ideas. Every experienced ideas person has a list somewhere of the ideas that didn't get through the selling process and didn't get made. There's a huge amount of effort that goes into generating new ideas. Therefore, there is value in keeping a note of those ideas that didn't quite make it, and seeing if they have value in a new context. This does not mean shoehorning an idea that does not fit. It isn't time for the Glass Slipper to be forced onto the foot of either stepsister. It does mean revisiting an idea that fell by the wayside and seeing if it can be built on to satisfy a new brief, audience or tech platform.

There is lots of rhetoric about the speed of change, but fundamentally nothing has changed. People are the same, human nature has not changed and we can produce great work only if we have true human insight for our professional target audiences (and for each other as teammates.)

Five hundred years ago the amount of information and data the average person was likely to see *in a whole year* probably equates to 60 minutes of scrolling through social media now. But our human brains haven't evolved in that time frame. Which is why we blank out and ignore nearly everything that we see and just retain the tiny amount that interests or entertains us.

Cutting through the clutter is more crucial as a skill than ever before for communication. A distinctive old idea, one that stirs us emotionally and triggers our memories, may well be a good place to start. Just as Hollywood continues to remake films, just as a cover version of an old hit can still have huge commercial success, keep referencing old hits and near misses. It might just be that there is a brilliant idea in the bank which could be perfect for your next creative opportunity.

Take Action

Could an old idea work for your current problem? Human nature hasn't changed that much, so something that worked in the past, but which has become old-fashioned, might work now. Find the person in your sector who has the most experience, and interview them about old techniques to see if anything is worth reviving. Keep a bank of the ideas that nearly happened but didn't quite make it, or that you tried, and could try again now that times have changed.

Work against your better judgement

The Portsmouth Sinfonia is an orchestra founded in 1970 by a group of students. The idea behind it was that you either didn't need to be expert in any instrument, or if you were a musician you had to play an instrument that was unfamiliar to you. The orchestra became notorious and made several records throughout that decade. The idea was not to play badly, but to play with enthusiasm and commitment. The rules stated that everyone had to turn up to rehearsals and play to their best ability. Clearly this goes against all the rules. Well, what if you get your best people together but ask them to change roles? Ask your team to play to their weaknesses for once instead of their strengths. Get the finance man to give his best gut instinct creative ideas, and ask your creative types to be analytical. Or simply make it clear that everyone needs a point of view on the topic whatever their key strengths. Sometimes naïve ideas are the best ones, just like 'stupid' questions are often the ones that get to the real issues.

In any business made for profit, giving stuff away may well seem madness at first. But this is the genius of the loss-leader. Many stores sell products at less than the price that it costs to produce them in order to entice customers into the stores to buy more expensive items. Usually loss-leaders are staple goods like milk or eggs. While shopping, the customer might then pick up an expensive item. So, selling stuff for less than the price of production might well go against your better judgement, but it is a long-standing proven technique for generating huge profits overall. There are some categories where all the profit and loyalty comes from the replacement of items. Think of printers. The real income comes from replacement cartridges. It makes sense to discount the cost of the printer in order to get customers for the replacement items. Brita water filters make their money from the replacement filters, not the original jugs which are frequently discounted. Many nightclubs have cheap or even free entry on some nights. Get the customers in, then make the margin on the drinks you sell them.

What can you give away in order to entice customers to buy more expensive products and services?

You can also get great ideas if you go against the better judgement that your personality dictates. One of your authors is a natural introvert and prefers to stay in most of the time. The other is a huge extrovert and goes out a lot. Working together we find that our differences mean that we get a balanced view of business. The introvert is made to go out more than she naturally would (our previous books have led to over 200 public speaking engagements). The extrovert has to sit, think and write more than she normally would. Working against our innate judgements has been good for both of us.

Sometimes the most random outcomes can come from going against your better judgement. Mickey Flanagan is a comedian whose most famous routine is the 'Out out' sketch, first performed in 2010. Here he defined the difference between going out to the shops for a pint of milk, for example, versus going 'out out' – often accidentally because you 'bump into a mate and you're still in the pub six hours later'. Going 'out out' could well be against your better judgement, but you might love it. Taking your team 'out out' could be the bonding exercise you all needed.

If you do go against your better judgement, take time to review the outcomes. It's great to use this technique to come up with ideas, but make sure you sleep on them before you go ahead.

Take Action

Go against your better judgement and try some ideas or some techniques that make you wince. But make sure that you check in with the wider team, and your own second thoughts, before you go any further with them.

Build back better

We're painfully aware that this phrase has been used as a policy framework and is slightly challenging – after all, who intentionally builds back badly? So, dear reader, forget the title and allow us to build back your interest in a more optimal way.

Building back better has its roots in policy in the United Nations, where the phrase was first used by President Bill Clinton, who wanted to introduce a policy that reduced the disaster risk to people and nations. From this start, *building back better* has changed into an approach that reduces risk to businesses too.

Even in start-up mode, there are company tenets in place from day one. But nothing is ever so fluid that there is no room for improvement. The key is for you to take what you have and use all the things available to you to ensure that you are able to use any setback, major or minor, to improve in the future. This is a much more constructive approach than just abandoning anything that doesn't work wholesale. Doing that might seem cathartic, but can create problems with colleagues; after all, they put a lot of effort and intensity into the project, and to dismiss everything associated with it can be demoralizing. Next time, will they be as invested and try so hard? Perhaps not, if they feel it will be dismissed out of hand without recognition.

So how do we build back better? It's important to recognize what worked and to celebrate that as a job well done. Balancing that, an unemotional and blame-free look at what didn't work is also required. Was it too rushed to be viable? Did we have the best processes in place? Do we need help from a new set of contributors? Be open and honest and, most of all, kind. If you run a process built on fear, no one will ever say when there is a concern, they will keep quiet and wait for things to fall apart. If you decide to operate a *good news only* information loop, cracks and then fissures and, finally, gaping holes will appear – and that isn't a viable way to build and grow a company. You cannot build without foundations. That sounds obvious, but there are numerous examples where the rush to start and the excitement of an idea meant that those involved forgot to create a sound structure.

It may sound obvious, but what would you keep from your previous process? Can it be reused or repurposed? It could be that the market isn't quite right for that idea at that time, so keep it, log it and make sure it's ready to go (or at least 90 per cent there) should the time be right. You can be too late to the market and so be behind – or you can be too early and be offering something that people don't want. At the moment.

If there isn't anything redeemable, it could be that your initial assumptions or workings were flawed, rather than the way you developed the idea. Clarity, and a realistic assessment of where you are and what the opportunity could be, are essential. You also need to be hard-nosed about what you can do in the time frame. Yes, you could change everything, but only if you employed 200 more people with a specific skill set that takes a while to learn and assimilate. No, that isn't possible – and for your own sake, please do accept that truth. Trust us, you will thank us for it. McKinsey identified in 2007 that executives quite often look in the wrong places for insights that will deliver an edge. Instead of reading about success stories or techniques that are based on questionable data, we're better off utilizing and developing our critical thinking. We can only build back better if we know what is possible, and the stories we read about crazy ideas that then went on to become market leaders attract attention precisely because they are the exception, and not the predictable outcome or the experience of most companies.

Take Action

You can build back better only if you acknowledge what is wrong. Corporate leaders sometimes shy away from this, just like politicians. It's easy to criticize other people, and harder to acknowledge how things can be better in your own work. Working out the specifics of what does need to change can be an inspirational springboard for creativity.

What would someone else say?

It's not a secret that we believe that diversity drives business growth. Our last book, *Belonging*, is packed full of reasons to promote diverse voices. It isn't just that it's good in terms of fairness. It drives commercial outcomes and is also crucial to creativity – and truly creative people, whoever they are, synthesize different voices to create powerful new work and ideas.

In 1963 Mike Nichols (who subsequently went on to direct and win an Oscar for *The Graduate*) was just about to embark on directing for the first time; he had been a comedy performer until then.

His first play, which he was expected to prepare in just five days, was *Barefoot in the Park* (later also a hit film). It was written by Neil Simon and starred Robert Redford in one of his breakthrough roles. Speaking on the Sky documentary 'Becoming Mike Nichols', Nichols talked about the process of creating the play, which included a lot of rewrites and improv – his preferred way of working.

New job, lots to prove, five-day turnaround – and the script unfinished. Quite a challenge. The play was funny, but it didn't have an ending, and though he and Simon wracked their brains they couldn't find a good third act. The breakthrough came from an older friend of Nichols who watched a rehearsal, the writer Lillian Hellman. She commented on one scene, saying that she had a much better idea for it. She suggested that the mother-in-law of the lead character played by Redford might sneak off with the rakish elderly gentleman who lived upstairs for a fling. Nichols eventually realized this was the twist that the play needed – the action that allowed the resolution of the stormy new marriage of the main plot.

Nichols, then closer in age to the young married couple who star in the show, couldn't imagine the mother-in-law (in her 50s) having illicit sex with the man upstairs. As he reminisced about it for the documentary, he sounded somewhat shocked even in retrospect. What was clear was that without Hellman, a woman in her late 50s, the thirty-something men who were writing and directing would neither have considered, let alone given themselves permission, to add this charming twist to the plot.

Nichols and Simon, two men in their thirties and stumped creatively, were saved by listening to the voice of a woman of an age that tends to make women fairly invisible in traditional creative departments.

As Stef Calcraft, global CEO of Creative Transformation at EssenceMediacom, has said: 'Here's to the creative ones, and that can be all of us.' If it isn't all of us, really all of us, in our full differences in every respect (including age), there just won't be as much creativity.

Take Action

Include diverse voices in your problem-solving. Who are your team, what are they like? Add some people who are completely different. Ask those who are firmly outside the loop what they think. And really listen to what they say.

Take a trip

Breaking out of the familiar can be invigorating. Think about your holidays – new scenery, new inspiration and a chance to reflect and renew. Work trips can also be a chance to reflect and renew, so next time you are on a flight with a colleague, forget about dealing with your inbox and have a proper talk about opportunities and what's next. Maybe only for 30 minutes or so, and make it clear that these sessions are about the future, not moaning about the location of the last office celebration. Set yourself a short session to do a *what if* or *even better if* blitz on an aspect of your work.

The other type of trip you can take is the one that your customers take. If you are looking to make a change, this can come from a number of areas – technical improvements, issues around supply of key elements, changes to the market or new challengers to your market position. Depending on your challenge, your trip will be different. If your market is changing – a diminishing customer base, for example – your trip will involve finding your potential new customers and finding out what changes you need to make to attract them.

If you're going anywhere, make it where your customers are. Or where you would like them to be.

First things first: how do they find you and what is your welcome like? It's easy to get familiar with what you offer, but make your trip one of discovery. You know when you're travelling and your diary means you turn up too early for check-in? We like it when they take your case and put it in your room when it's ready – and you don't have to take a ticket, come back after a long day of meetings and maybe dinner, and then hang around while the one person still in reception retrieves your belongings at 11 p.m. Especially when it's 11 p.m. and there is no sign of anyone in reception. Make it easy and make it simple. You want these people, your customers, to choose you again and again, above any of your competitors.

The other great thing about trips are your memories. What memories do you leave your customers with? Good, bad or indifferent? Or, even worse, they can't remember you at all?

There is an element of a trip where the familiar offers a comfort – you know the good restaurants, the best beaches, the nicest place for ice cream. However, the familiar can start to feel a little overfamiliar and dull after a while. What new elements can you bring to your market? They don't have to be big – it could be a one-off test product you'd like them to try as part of a select group. In this age of email, it can be tempting to feel that frequency of communication is nirvana. It isn't. It's like being on holiday in the same location with a group that have decided are going to be your friends. They ask your plans and they follow you there. Place themselves next to you at breakfast when you just want to ease into your day. They say that going on holiday is a test of friendship. Make sure your client trip is one they'd like to repeat and that you're still talking at the end.

It's also worth exploring, via a trip, other markets and how they do things. This can offer a lot of insight on what to do and what not to do. It goes without saying that cultural and societal norms affect the products on offer, so don't assume anything from what you see. Take the elements that appeal and see if they fit your market, whether you could take it and make it work. Play with it and see what your market interpretation is.

What we're looking for when we take a trip is the chance to see what's possible and how new perspectives can help us. It may be that your trip takes you to a place where you never thought you would go.

Take Action

Go on, get away from it all. Explore, break the norms and immerse the team in a completely unfamiliar situation.

Be more *Wimbledon*

John McEnroe is famous, particularly in the UK, for being outspoken. Back in 1981, a young John McEnroe, sporting a headband and frizzy hair, was so furious at the refusal by the Wimbledon umpire Edward James to rule his serve in that he uttered the immortal line: 'You cannot be serious' before subjecting the Centre Court crowd to a tirade of ill-tempered invective. The country erupted in outrage. And it remains an iconic moment in tennis.

In the corporate world, some people find speaking bluntly difficult. McEnroe's view was that he was the 'normal' one on the tennis court. As he explained in the documentary *McEnroe*, released in 2022: 'What I've always thought about myself is that I'm more like the normal guy than Björn [Borg] is,' he explains. 'Björn's the freak that could go out there and not change his expression for four hours. I'm the normal guy that gets frustrated on the court and expresses himself.'

He believed in winning at any cost, but goes on to say that 37 therapists didn't help him really be normal.

Is anyone who is world-beating entirely 'normal'? Not by definition.

Is it possible to win without ranting? Yes, of course.

Has psyching out your opponent become common practice? Yes, of course.

Can you give robust feedback without upsetting people? Undoubtedly. In our book from 2016, *The Glass Wall: success strategies for women at work – and businesses that mean business*, one highly successful contributor explains how to give criticism so that it is well received: 'Above all, I am authentic. I would say that what I do is the Shit Sandwich. I'm quite nice to people, I try and be understanding and empathetic and listen, but it doesn't stop me from confronting what's wrong. Nice, and then I'll be horrible. But then I'll say I love you, let's have lunch. I get furious, but then I say, it's only work, there are more important things, let's make friends.'

However, this is **not** how we should be more *Wimbledon*.

And it's **not** by eating more strawberries and cream, or drinking more Pimms.

We should be more *Wimbledon* by adopting the rule of the second serve.

The genius of the tennis game lies in the second serve.

What other game, or profession, authorizes you to make your best shot with no worry of failure? In tennis every player can shoot for the moon with their first serve, with no anxiety at all about it missing.

Imagine how much more interesting (to my mind – apologies to the football purists) penalty shoot-outs would be under these rules, where every shooter would get two shots at goal. Imagine what this would do to our education system if a brave go was written into some subjects. Think how you would feel in a pitch or answering a client brief if the rule was to go twice – first you shoot for the moon, then you give a safety shot.

Of course, we all have the option to give a range of solutions. But that's different, that's about options not ambition. The *second serve* rule should be baked in, and I would recommend to any client giving a brief today that they try this as mandatory and see what that does to the responses.

Business is transforming thanks to the advent of AI and automation. Efficient automation levels the playing field in mature markets, and means that competitive advantage lies in those businesses that fuel differentiation with creativity.

The *second serve* rule can transform that creativity.

Take Action

Come up with ideas as if you don't care whether they fail or what the consequences are. Observe the *second serve* rule and reach for the stars. Work on the basis that you have two shots, and give your first shot everything.

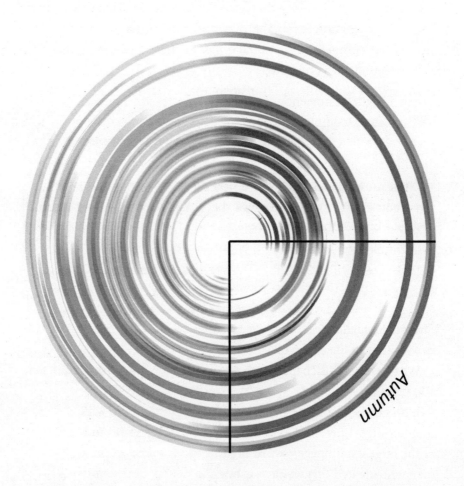

Autumn

CHAPTER FIVE

Autumn – the fall, the rise, the revolution

When insight is not enough to deliver a creative solution, it might be time for a complete revolution. This might mean adopting new practices, restructuring the team, re-examining the goals of the project, or building a new community spirit at work. Many plans for change fail because workplaces have a strong muscle memory of how things work. They reject the new in favour of *we've always done it this way*, and despite a brainstorm of ideas revert to the comfort zone of conformity with the status quo. In making organizational changes stick, there are steps to take to facilitate the adoption of new ways of working; you need to prepare the path to acceptance of creativity and revolution. If you're going to get a new heart and spirit of change, then you need to discard, like fallen leaves, the issues and practices that might mean the new chance of life and rebirth is rejected.

We will open this chapter with a revolutionary story from more than 100 years ago.

John Lewis is a business that is over a century old and which, despite that heritage, operates a way of working that resonates today. It's one of the largest employee-owned organizations in the world and yet the man who created this vision was born in the late 19th century.

John Spedan Lewis started work for his father, the original John Lewis, when he was 19. His father was the owner of the well-known John Lewis store in Oxford Street and when John Spedan Lewis was 21, he inherited 25 per cent of the company. The realization that he, his father and his brother collectively earned more than the entire number of employees changed him. 'It is wrong to have millionaires before you have ceased to have slums,' he said. Introducing a partnership model, where all the employees own the business, was his creative approach to both his business and his colleagues. Today, John Lewis says of itself that it is to all intents and purposes a social enterprise model, with all the profits that they make reinvested for the benefit of both customers and employees. Except they aren't employees, they are partners – in the business and with their customers. (John Lewis doesn't allow partners to upsell: if you go to them and say you want, say, a television and your budget is £800, they will find you the best television for your needs for £800. They won't try to get you to spend more so that they make more cash or hit a sales target.)

In a similar stance, all pay levels are relative. The Managing Director is limited to a specific multiple of the average median pay. So, no huge disparity here between the shop floor people and the senior management. This behaviour is inherent in the business, with John Lewis introducing free healthcare for employees 19 years before the National Health Service came into being. After 25 years' service, you get six months' fully paid leave as a sabbatical. There are five hotels owned by the partnership that partners and their invited guests can enjoy. Radical? Perhaps. But as an article in the *Guardian* by Gemma Goldfingle said in March 2023, 'it is precisely this model that makes customers so loyal, John Lewis and Waitrose shoppers could buy cheaper beans, bread or bras elsewhere, but there is an inherent trust in the retailer that is tied up in its ownership structure.'

It's interesting that an organization which has existed for over 100 years has a constitution that requires them to make 'sufficient' profit but not the maximum possible. This is of particular relevance in a world where short-term market considerations can drive business decisions. If you're close to your financial year end as a company, the need to make your balance sheet look good might mean you delay a piece of capital investment that then puts you at a disadvantage to a competitor: they invested and deployed earlier than you, so you are playing catch-up. In some instances, median pay goes down (pressure on margins and profit squeeze invoked as the reasons) while the senior team (whose bonuses are linked to share price maintenance or improvement) appear to make more money than ever. In a time when attracting people to work with us for a long time appears increasingly difficult, the approach of John Spedan Lewis looks visionary, even though the rapidly changing world of shopping has created new challenges for the store.

Of course, not many people are in a position to work for a company that is employee-owned or a social enterprise, so what does the John Lewis model mean for us, and how does it prompt us to think creatively about where we work and how we work? In essence, it is the belief and the delivery of a company that is people-focused, with a set of values and beliefs that drive employee/partner behaviour but which are also clearly valuable to consumers. Let's think about the people delivering the ideas that we have and how that translates into how our customers feel.

John Lewis is a business that has survived much change. It has new challenges now, but it is a remarkable example of an organization that broke the accepted practices of its time, and put its people first.

The ideas in this chapter are about how to look at working practices in a new way, and to rip up the old tired ways. We will start with how you organize for success, not for immediate impact, not for long-term impact but for the medium term. This is not often how things are judged, so what if you think about outcomes in this way?

Organize for medium-term success
Make it famous, fast
Build communities
Make the team happy
Be generous
Build bridges

Make people's lives better

Deliver outstanding teamwork

What is missing?

Harvest

Listen hard

Do things in the wrong order

What would your worst enemy do?

Organize for medium-term success

The medium term gets a bad press – it's not reactive and tactical enough to get your pulse racing and your adrenaline pumping and neither is it going to leave the legacy we expect of the long term. It's kind of a beige choice as if you can't be bothered to make a real effort. *I'm aiming for medium-term success* isn't a phrase we hear in job interview responses.

However, organizing for the medium term can have benefits for teams. It removes the pressure of a quick fix, of *do it now and get it done.* It also doesn't have the burden of trying to find a long-term, big idea that is the answer to everything, even questions that haven't come up yet.

Organizing for the medium term can grant you a level of freedom that you weren't expecting, while also removing the barrier we inadvertently erect by rating the concepts and ideas that we produce. This barrier – justified at times – is our reluctance to adopt the obvious ideas and solutions. It would take a far more qualified author than either of us to explain the psychology behind this aversion to the obvious, but these are some of the thoughts we've had. All too often our problem-solving or creativity is burdened by the notion that getting to the idea must be hard, wrangled out of us by hours of hard work and pondering. Putting ideas out and pulling them apart until we find the ultimate idea. Anything that feels obvious gets ignored because it is so . . . obvious. The longer that we ignore the obvious, the more hard-baked the aversion to it is, as if we believe that it must be wrong. Otherwise, why didn't we do the obvious before? So we assume it's already been analysed and dismissed – and so another layer of resistance to that solution develops. It is strange how hard-baked these beliefs and behaviours become in companies.

If we organize for the medium term, we can afford to embrace the obvious. It will help us quickly address any pressing issues and acts as a bridge to the next push of ideas and creativity.

Organizing for the medium term gives teams the chance of a get-out emotionally and psychologically. The pressure for the transformation is so much less when the expected time frame is shorter. You also get the benefit of not having to anticipate what key elements will be needed in the very longer term. The only thing we know that never changes is the fact that everything changes and sometimes more quickly than you had anticipated – being organized for the medium term gives you a flexibility that a five-year plan might not. If you want to be nimble, maybe medium is the right stance for you.

If medium is your start point, it may be that you change your approach to a number of contributing factors that affect the process. Resources and money can both be barriers to solutions. In organizing for the medium term, your resources can be evaluated in a different way – you can either decide to stretch existing resources to cover the plan, or you can choose a more flexible, freelance or fixed-term resource. On money, as you aren't committing to the long term, your fixed requirements may not be as burdensome, and so you can invest more upfront, knowing that there is a return coming in the not too distant future. By avoiding the notion that you're tied in for the long term, and that you are building a sustainable project, you may be able more easily to access the cash needed to get the job done.

Medium doesn't have to mean that something isn't finished – view the development as a staircase, building upwards steadily and mindfully.

Take Action

Don't worry about the short-term impact of the task in hand, and don't think about a long-term effect either. Think about things that are immediate barriers to overcome, and don't worry (for now) about the long-term consequences. Brief the team to ensure that they are not constrained by short-term impact – there's likely to be muscle memory that prompts them to focus on this, which so often means that if something doesn't deliver in the short term, it is cancelled. Set your sights on the mid horizon.

Make it famous, fast

And now, by contrast, think about fast outcomes. In 1967, when Andy Warhol (possibly) said 'In the future everyone will be famous for 15 minutes', fame was a lot harder to come by.

In those days you had to reach the attention of the minority who were the gatekeepers of fame. That might be by appearing on a TV talent show (famous UK examples include *New Faces*, won by the 16-year-old comedian Lenny Henry, and *Opportunity Knocks*, which made a star of the poet and comedian Pam Ayres) or a variety show such as *The Ed Sullivan Show* in the United States, which created overnight stardom for Elvis Presley, Dusty Springfield and the Beatles.

Now algorithms act as gatekeepers to fame instead. If you can go viral on social media, you can get an income and become famous – at least for a while.

Wherever you require a creative leap, one way of reaching it is by asking the question: *How can we make this famous, fast?*

So how can we acquire fame? You need to tap into popular culture. This might be by jumping into the latest fad on social media. It could be by leveraging a deep-rooted human drive.

Latest trends are easy enough to find. About 2,000,000,000 results come up when you search for the subject. Pick one of the top five and try making it relevant to your issue. There are some trends that persist. Cute puppies and dancing dogs always trend well. Lip-synching never gets tired and cats falling off things has been an internet trend since the earliest days. Pinterest predictions for 2024 included Grandpa chic; small aquarium gardens; jellyfish haircuts; a badminton craze; and heading for the mountains.

Trending on social media mostly does not just happen. Influencers are users on social media who have established credibility in a specific industry. These content creators can have access to a large audience and can share information to persuade others through their authenticity and reach. The individuals in question work hard to build and maintain their followings. One way to build fame fast is to reach out to those who already reach your audience and offer them remuneration in terms of product or pay in order to get their endorsement. Or find a social media user in your circle and engage them to build a set of followers for you.

You can also find fame if you can tap into a deep-rooted human drive. In 2000, the University of Ohio produced a study listing 16 basic human drives: power, independence, curiosity, acceptance, order, saving, honour, idealism, social contact, family, status, vengeance, romance/sex, eating, physical exercise, and tranquillity.

In the 1990s UK ad shop The Media Business found fame fast when a research study into what housewives thought about advertising garnered headlines through a press release highlighting one additional question. Sue, who had conducted the research, also asked the respondents to the study whether they'd prefer sex with their husband or a shopping voucher. The answers were definitive: the voucher, along with time alone to go shopping, was by far the preferred choice. This made headlines in several national newspapers, including the front pages, and was picked up in the United States by the *National Enquirer*. The fame didn't last, but it did help the agency attract new business. The study was a serious one, about the lack of connection that women overall felt with most advertising. But by spinning off a story to attract press attention, by tapping into the obsession that the tabloids had and still have about sex and the housewife, the level of fame spiralled.

Take Action

Tap into the basic human drives or spin off the latest internet trends to build fame fast for your business ideas. Look at https://trends.google.com/trends/; consider what is trending on TikTok and X (formerly Twitter); or look for inspiration in the deep human drives which never change: Maslow's hierarchy of needs, and the Ohio University list above.

Build communities

What's creativity for?

One use is creative destruction. To destroy and to clear away old and legacy models, enabling you to create new mores and standards. Sometimes it is impossible to create the new if the heritage of the past hangs heavily on your organization or culture.

If this is your intention, building a community can enable you to get support from the crowd – and it's a good place to start.

For many millennia your community meant a local community in real life within a few miles of where you were born. Most people knew the same people all their lives, for good or bad, and stayed in touch. It was only really in the second half of the twentieth century that family units became smaller and more independent, and it became more of the norm to move away from friends and family and from your place of birth. Urban landscapes changed so that you didn't stay in contact constantly with your neighbours. In fact, especially in London, you might never meet them. Modern life became weird.

With the internet came social media, which enabled communities to be reinvented. Friends Reunited, MySpace, Second Life and, of course,

Facebook allowed human beings to fulfil a deep-rooted emotional need to connect. A child of the millennium can stay in touch with everyone they were at school with all their lives – should they wish to, that is. As contact has grown, so too has ghosting.

Social media also allowed people with passions to connect. Until this flourishing in the early twenty-first century, you might have a passion for collecting or a geeky interest in a niche topic but you were pretty much on your own unless you found a club in real life to join. If your passions were niche, the chances of this were minimal before Twitter, Pinterest and Instagram gave us communities of interest around anything you can think of, from cookies and quilting to independent bookshops.

Of course, before social media there were other ways to pursue your passions, and magazines thrived from feeding them. The writer and commentator John Grant has called them *catalogues of passion*, not simply paper and print. They allowed people to connect with people they didn't know in real life who shared their interests, and this was (and is) enriching on a personal and a creative level.

People with passions are curious about their topic (unceasingly). People with passions connect despite other differences of age, class, gender, race, sexuality, even politics. They connect across barriers. And if you can create communities that are passionate about your business, it can step-change your profitability.

People with passions can create (and also destroy). If you can harness this, you can step-change the success of your project, venture or brand.

Justine Roberts is the co-founder of Mumsnet, a social media platform that gave a voice to the silent. If an idea catches hold there, it makes national news. Her community famously gave UK Prime Minister Gordon Brown a tough time because he was unable to name his favourite biscuit. The Mumsnet community can create success and failures. As Roberts once said: 'If they like your ideas, then they will tell everyone; and if they don't, then they will tell everyone that too.'

The #metoo and @everydaysexism communities on X (formerly Twitter) have created new societal norms where silent millions have gained a voice and wielded power.

TikTok, Instagram, Pinterest and the rest all deliver communities and connections. If you're facing a situation that needs change and creativity, reach out to or create a new community and harness the power of the people.

Take Action

Ask yourself and your team how you can get a community to rally behind your cause. This could be a physical community, or a community of passions. Within your organization there may be communities that will be enthusiastic about the next challenge, reach out to them.

Make the team happy

You aren't here to be happy, you're here to do your work, said nobody who ever wanted people to commit to the task in hand. We're fully aware that some people's idea of happiness at work is to have a ping-pong league, complete with a handicapping system so that it's more equitable, which they think is going to be enormous fun. Or to go out for drinks every time an opportunity presents itself: 'George finally managed to use the coffee machine without setting off a fire alarm – that calls for Martinis across the team, doesn't it?'

Work happiness means different things to different people, but our premise is that happier people deliver better results. By putting your people first, you create a virtuous circle where they deliver more and are happy because their work is great. Great work makes people want to do more great work, so the happiness grows and *OK, look what's happened, we're all enjoying work a whole lot more.* Research that was published in Forbes suggests that happy employees are up to 20 per cent more productive than those that are unhappy. Other sources suggest that workplace happiness improves sales, productivity and accuracy.

Feeling that who you are matters is an important factor. So when we're setting up our creative taskforces, we should consider how we frame the way we introduce and position our participants. 'Nickie is here to make sure we don't get sent to prison, so be careful what you say in front of her!' is one way to introduce Nickie, but it does make her look like a grumpy killjoy and also implies that she has nothing else to contribute than a gloomy presence, as someone who will smother even the faintest risk. There is an equal pressure in lauding someone for a talent: 'Sue is the cleverest person in the room, so we'll be fine.' (Sue is indeed very, very clever, but that implies everyone else can kick back and do nothing, and puts undue focus on her. It also means that you might be creating a cohort who do nothing but find ways to decimate her ideas.)

'This is Kurt, he's here representing IT: he's got experience in CSR management and intuitive customer systems.' That may be all I need to know about Kurt right now. Or is it? Do I know what intuitive customer systems are and could someone explain why that might be useful for this project?

So, we set our teams up and make them feel valued. We then talk about the impact the work we're doing will have. This can be as simple as making our internal processes easier to navigate or any other benefit that might be the outcome. Make the team feel that this process has value – to the business, to the employees or to the end customer. No one wants to feel that it's just a process. Very few people are motivated by process unless that process adds something. Finally, try to ensure that by taking part in the creative change, people are able to learn something. This works in two ways – the participants feel they have gained something and their managers are more willing to allow colleagues to take part if they come back with a wider skill set or piece of knowledge.

How you put together your team is a key element for success and participant happiness. Watching the drama unfold as two team members break into open conflict may have its appeal, but we're here to deliver something, not create reality TV, so be mindful if you're told that X doesn't really work well with Y. Just accept that and find another combination. Similarly, while we all need a reality check, don't add a professional cynic/complainer to your team. Recognize that their boss might be volunteering them to give everyone they work with day to day a break – so just say no. Healthy scepticism and perspective is good; continual moaning isn't.

Take Action

Keep a check on the happiness levels of the team. Dips are fine, ravines of misery aren't. Have some ideas about what you can do to keep your happiness high. This might be as simple as consulting them on what would make them happy. It will involve empowering them, giving them purpose and new skills.

Be generous

If you are looking for a creative idea, try being generous.

This works in two different ways.

Physically: Be generous with size

If you're selling clothes, being generous with sizes is proven to sell to more women. In 2010 the Social Science Research Network published a study that proved that women prefer smaller size labels; perhaps unsurprisingly this boosts their mental image of themselves. Journalist Eliana Dockterman has a theory that as the weight of the average American woman rose from 140lb (64kg) in 1960 to 168lb (76kg) in 2014, brands adjusted their metrics to help women fit into smaller sizes, creating an arms race as competitive brands all tried to be more generous than each other. So, a size 8 in one brand might be a size 12 in another. And let's be honest, we prefer to buy a size 8 if we can. Apply this to your challenge – boost the customer's self-esteem by being generous with sizes. This doesn't just involve clothes. It means working out what a super-efficient offering is, and then adding in some leeway to your business plan. You might offer some incentive for returning customers, such as a free coffee with every fifth visit. A partnership with a business sharing your purpose could be helpful – is there a supermarket loyalty scheme that you could join, or a brand partnership which is mutually beneficial?

Emotionally: Be generous; get good karma

Behaving generously is at the heart of most religious theory. Doing good deeds and reaping a reward is the basis of the fairy tales we tell children.

The heroes of stories who stumble across an old woman in the woods will interrupt their adventure to help her collect firewood. In return they will receive an apparently worthless item which will turn out to be a supernatural intervention that saves their life and aids their mission.

Kindness and warmth can get you further than aggression and forcefulness. Aesop's fable 'The North Wind and the Sun' demonstrates this. The sun and the wind are arguing about who is more powerful. They decide on a challenge: which of them can remove the coat from the back of a man walking beneath? The wind blows hard and then harder. The more powerfully it blows, the tighter the man clutches his coat. The sun shines warmly on the man, so much so that he removes his coat, surprised at the change in the weather. How can your generosity cause a warmer climate in your organization, or for your customer?

Professionally it is always relevant to be as kind and generous as you can to those who need your help. When the tables are turned, you'll be happy to have this reciprocated. If you have something that might help someone else – a book, a name, an experience – or that might benefit them, give it freely. Don't save up you favours for when you'll get a quick payback; play the long game.

In business, people sometimes get sceptical of generosity and pursue the selfish option. Culture leads us to believe that this is the normal way, with hit dramas like *Succession* and (back in the day) *Dynasty or Dallas*. It just isn't true. The social psychologist Jonathan Haidt says that human behaviour is shaped mostly by being descended from apes, but that we are also behaviourally part bee.

The ape part of us propels us to try and get to the top of the tree. We are pack animals, and we want the approval of the alpha boss. Haidt writes: 'We've been told for years now that human beings are fundamentally selfish. We're assaulted by reality TV programmes showing people at their worst . . . It's not true. We may spend most of our working hours advancing our own interests, but we all have the capacity to transcend self-interest and become part of a whole.'

Could your creative idea transcend self-interest and promote the health of the whole hive?

Take Action

Act with generosity in your heart and find an idea that exceeds expectations. This might mean adapting your product offering to ensure that the customer is delighted and surprised by its generosity. It could mean a partnership with another brand to reward loyalty. It might mean ensuring that you are helping others in your work life. Bread scattered on the waters now will always pay back.

Build bridges

It's fairly obvious that a coherent team is the best way to progress ideas, and our instinct is to create a team that represents the various stakeholders in the idea or project we're trying to develop. So you have a person from finance, marketing, logistics, etc. and you all sit in a room and try to work together on something that might not exist yet. Sounds reasonable, but it's very hard to make anything happen if one of your participants doesn't want to be there and another who has taken an instant dislike to someone else in the team. (We exaggerate for effect, but at some point one of your authors sat in an ideas generation session where after two hours we couldn't even agree the name for the project team. It wasn't a career highlight, especially as we carried on for three hours. Without finding a name we all agreed on, we chose to move to a less contentious topic.)

By building bridges between the team, we can achieve much more. Start by having everyone talk about why they are there, what they hope to bring to the project and how they like to work. This is key. If you are a person who likes to work things through in a quiet and steady way, being in the middle of a free-for-all brainstorm won't make you comfortable. You will be reluctant to express yourself and so your input will be lost. Finding a way for an introverted and logical perspective to be showcased adds a dimension that is needed so that the idea is fully tested and robust. The personalities and qualities that we bring into the room shape what comes out. You need to populate the team carefully and with consideration.

The writer Lucy Prebble, part of the team that created the TV series *Succession* to great acclaim, talked about her initial approach to pitching her script ideas. 'When I would pitch early on, I would preface it by saying "This is rubbish but", thus making everyone sit through an idea I had told them was shit. It took me time to realize I was not only instructing people not to listen to me, but also wasting time.' If you're asking your colleagues to come up with ideas, make sure that you don't confuse being articulate with having the best option. Build a bridge so that all of the perspectives that could create a compelling idea are able to be brought forward. Encourage those people who are great advocates for ideas to articulate the ideas of those who aren't as comfortable. For those participants who are great at ideas but not good at detail, find a work buddy who can help them flesh the idea out fully, with the detail and depth that you need.

You should also consider building bridges internally, outside of your working team. Who would be a great pair of new eyes to look at your work in progress and give you constructive and helpful advice? Is there anyone who has started a new initiative that might give you help? If you're the team leader, don't keep these conversations to yourself. Ask those people to come and talk to the working group as a whole – that way, everyone in the group hears the feedback and can process it. This also avoids any team leader reacting to the feedback as a personal affront and ignoring the elements they don't like. The best outcomes are those that are honed by the group and shaped by advice, not the isolated and inverted product of a bunch of people who never worked collectively. By building bridges we can encourage our teams to think differently and share skills. Build confidence in their capabilities and deliver ideas that work.

Take Action

Reach out to others and build connections. Ensure that the team is indeed a team and not a set of talented individuals. Where there is disharmony, energy is expended on the wrong activities and good thinking is misdirected. Consider yourself Chief Bridge Builder, and engineer harmony.

Make people's lives better

Peru is one of the most macho countries in the world, according to Charlie Tolmas, the Chief Creative Officer at advertising agency Circus Grey in Lima. Lack of education, and social norms, means that women frequently do not have the same economic opportunities as men. According to Statista, women in Peru are over a third less likely than men to access equal opportunities at work. They are therefore much more likely to be dependent on men.

Circus Grey was faced with the challenge of creating a campaign for their client Mibanco, a financial services business that specializes in loans to start-ups. Tolmas' team could easily have come up with a whole range of adverts that offered good rates or easy access.

Instead, they worked with the bank to make women's lives better.

In the Peruvian financial system, banks have a policy that a married woman wanting to take out a loan needs her husband's signature. This is mandatory, and he can simply refuse to sign. This can sometimes lead to a life of coercive control, in a nation where there is frequent violence against women. (In 2006 the World Health Organization reported that 69 per cent of Peruvian women had suffered some form of physical violence in their lives.)

Mibanco changed the loan form. They removed the space for a husband's signature and instead treated every woman applying for a loan as if she were single. Simple and profound. The business, with 300 branches across the country, found a creative way to promote their services by making women's lives a little better.

In 2021 online retailer eBay partnered with UK reality ITV hit *Love Island*. In a first for the genre, eBay promoted pre-loved fashion (that is, second-hand clothes). The show had had fashion sponsors in the past, and in fact in 2018 the online retailer Missguided had pioneered selling the outfits worn by the contestants instantly to viewers, seeing sales spike by 40 per cent. The team behind eBay's marketing subverted this, and instead provided the contestants with pre-loved outfits, and saw huge spikes to the pre-loved fashion sales on the site. Lindsey Jordan, Head of Creative Strategy at EssenceMediacom, worked on the idea with eBay's Marketing Chief Eve Williams. The team believe fundamentally in the importance of taking action for sustainability and in the mission of creating circularity in fashion where the full life of an item of clothing is considered – from the sustainability of materials through to what happens to the garment after its first owner has finished with it. There's huge growth in the UK in pre-loved clothes, and clearly the renaming of this trend has been key. One in five shoppers have at least one pre-loved item in their wardrobe. But until this campaign the trend was relatively low profile.

Eve Williams made clear that the intention was to flip the conversation around fashion. 'As one of the original homes of pre-loved, we believe that by joining forces with this incredibly influential programme, we'll inspire the nation to think differently and make more conscious choices when it comes to their wardrobes. Whether that is selling a dress that is sitting at the back of their wardrobe or shopping for their favourite islanders' second-hand looks – these small changes can make a big difference to driving circularity.'

The intention once again was to make people's lives better, and the outcome, again, was to drive business sales.

This is not about marketing or advertising. It is about the whole business of business. Societal leadership is now a core function of business. According to the 2024 Edelman Trust survey, an annual global research study of 32,000 respondents in 28 countries, 62 per cent of people now expect business leaders to manage changes in society, not only in their business. And business is the only remaining trusted institution, as 79 per cent of people trust their employer, and trust in media and government has fallen.

Finding a way to make lives better is not only a morally and ethically good thing to do, it is also a great pragmatic way to find great staff, to keep them, to attract good publicity and to grow sales.

Take Action

Look for a way that your business can contribute to making someone's life a little better, or work for social or environmental good. This might not need to be something big, that impacts society at large. It could be in your local community. Don't just

> think about what your product and service literally is, but what
> benefit it gives to those who purchase or use it. This might give
> you and your team ideas about marketing that go beyond where
> you are now and help you see the bigger picture. Can you amplify
> this and make it the core of what you create?

Deliver outstanding teamwork

This is a different creative technique from making the team happy, and
it owes a lot to sport.

In any great team, people need to understand their roles, play to their
strengths, be organized, communicate and sometimes step outside
their own comfort zone to secure success and support each other. Most
importantly of all, especially if there's a problem that needs solving
creatively, they need to be committed to each other and to feel safe.

The American football coaching legend Vince Lombardi said:
'Individual commitment to a group effort is what makes a team work, a
company work, a society work, a civilization work . . . people who work
together will win, whether it be against complex football defences, or
the problems of society.'

In 2009 Sue found herself in a swimming pool with the Barcelona
football club. The team was resting between two friendly matches at
Wembley (a friendly is a game played for its own sake, and not in a
league or competition). She was swimming at a hotel pool, which was
more crowded than usual, and the only other people were men, who
between swimming and using the jacuzzi and sauna, jumped into
green wheelie bins. Asking what was going on, she was told that this
was Barcelona's first team, and the wheelie bins were full of ice so that
they could have ice baths between saunas. (She was able to share the
pool and jacuzzi, but they kept the ice baths to themselves!)

Impressed to have been swimming with some of the best
footballers in the world (Lionel Messi and Andrés Iniesta), she

became keen to explore what it is about their strategy as a team that makes them so good.

Obviously, it helps to have some of the greatest football players in the world on your team, but lots of teams had great individual players and didn't do as well as the Barcelona team of this era, then arguably one of the best teams in the world. Of course, as these things go, the players who had the most attention were their goalscorers. But the players who made the team so good as a team, who made it all come together, were the midfielders Xavi and Iniesta. They were always available to receive a pass, and they immediately passed the ball on. A Barcelona player therefore always had someone to pass the ball to, the team was able to focus on staying in possession, and no one even had to boot the ball up the field in the hope that someone would be there to grab it. The *receive, pass, offer* system worked strongly to ensure that they didn't lose possession of the ball. Without the ball, the opposing team cannot score. If you played for Barcelona at its peak there was always someone to pass the ball back to, so you didn't run the risk of being the idiot who lost possession to the striker from the other team who went on to score the winning goal. Not everyone has to be or should be a goalscorer – a point that is just as true in the workplace.

There is always the danger in the workplace that the key dealmakers, or the pitch winners, or the high-profile leaders will look like the only reason for success or failure. But a team that plays as a team, where there is always someone available to take the ball or to receive a pass, will beat a team relying on a couple of star performers, no matter how brilliant.

Former Barcelona president Joan Laporta said about the club: 'Football is all about the collective. Solidarity is even more important though at Barcelona than anywhere else.'

Creating a culture where everyone is playing for the team and is ready to help their colleagues is even more essential in the dog-eat-dog environment of this uncertain economic environment.

Every business and every team benefits from the kind of psychological safety that the Barcelona team at its best represented.

Create an environment where there is always someone to pass the ball back to, and people will be braver in their creativity.

Take Action

Structure your team so that there is always a safety net – a culture of psychological safety, enabling members to step outside of comfort zones and experiment and innovate, is crucial for idea generation. Individuals are less likely to put their heads above the parapet if the consequence is negative. Create a set of rules of engagement for any idea generation, which includes positivity and reward for both giving an opinion and challenging the status quo. Build on each other's ideas and thoughts rather than say what is wrong with them.

What is missing?

In 1999, as the last century trickled to a close, Adam Morgan published *Eating The Big Fish: How Challenger Brands Can Compete Against Brand Leaders*.

One of the techniques in his bestselling book was called Intelligent Naivety. It's a complicated name for asking very simple questions. The kinds of questions that you forget to ask, or are too embarrassed to ask, when you are close to a business or know lots about the category. Morgan states that this is essential to number two businesses because they need a new way in. One example is Virgin Atlantic. A big competitor in the UK is British Airways – the flag carrier for the nation. For transatlantic flights they were the premier choice for comfort and service. Virgin sought parity in these two crucial areas, but they also created, and led with, in-flight entertainment innovation, being the first airline to introduce seatback screens across all classes so that every passenger could watch their own choice of entertainment. Before this there were big screens showing everyone the same film. People weren't dissatisfied with this, but the option of a smaller screen and personal selection, and the ability to change from one film to another if bored, delivered a product advantage for the airline. Virgin created a space in the market by looking for what wasn't there.

There are two techniques that we use for looking for what isn't there.

One is asking 'stupid' questions. In most meetings most people will do anything to avoid doing this. They might have lost track of the jargon and don't want to be seen to be out of the loop. They might hold their seniority and status too heavily (in our opinion the most important people in the meeting are not those with the most important title, but those people who have the best ideas). They might be too junior, and worried about interrupting the flow with a 'stupid' question. Those questions are often the most valuable.

Copywriter Dave Trott (the man behind great ads such us 'Lipsmackin' thirstquenchin' acetastin'. . . fastlivin' evergivin' Pepsi' and 'Hello Tosh, gotta Toshiba' among many others), used to ask his team to come up with ideas for a campaign before they'd read the brief providing details about the product. He wanted to hear what his team thought from the point of view of the general public, not the experts. He has written in praise of the 'stupid question' in his books (which include *Creative Mischief* and *Crossover Creativity*) saying:

> 'How much weaker is it to pretend to know when we don't?
> It seems to me to take a lot more confidence to say **'I don't know.'**
> Then at least I've got a chance of finding out.
> Also it's honest.
> And honesty is always stronger than lies.
> Keep quiet and hope everyone thinks we're intelligent.
> Which is what most people do.'

There is huge power in asking a question when everyone else is afraid to, and it might just unlock the truth that no one else has seen, and find the thing that is missing.

The second technique for finding what is missing is to start asking *Why?*, and importantly *Why not?* – and don't stop asking these questions till you find it.

Michael Dell, the founder of Dell Technologies and now a billionaire and philanthropist, told the three authors of *The Innovator's DNA* that he simply asked a question: *Why should a computer cost five times more than the sum of its parts?* Clearly there's a big enough profit margin at much less than this, evidenced by the fact that we're writing this on a Dell laptop. The authors – Clayton Christensen, Jeff Dyer and Hall Gregersen – pointed out that most managers tend to ask *How* questions: *How are we going to speed up this process? How are we going to be more efficient?* This might drive optimization, but it does not usually get you to new thinking. Asking *Why?* and *Why not?* can take you to uncharted territory.

Innovation takes you to the blue ocean, the uncharted territory, while your competitors remain in the red ocean of the traditional category norms. When Nintendo launched the Wii Fit in 2007, they stepped outside of the competitive set of action games and found a new audience in women seeking fitness, with games that included yoga and balance. As early purchasers for this game ourselves, we didn't know we were missing it until it arrived. Did Nintendo ask, *Why aren't more women buying our product?* If so, the question, and the game, step-changed the success of the business at launch.

Take Action

Look for what is missing and what is not there by asking naïve questions, asking stupid questions, asking *Why?*, then *Why?* again, then *Why not?*. Go where the competition is not present, and ask: *What would we gain by extending here?*

Harvest

The harvest may appear a strange construct for a book about creativity, but it can be a crucial step to creating your next successful project. Rather like in farming or gardening, you can use this time to celebrate what you have achieved and review what worked and what didn't – you, in effect, are sorting the wheat (what you want) from the chaff (what you don't want).

While you are basking in the glow of what you've achieved, it's time to take a cool look at what went into the success and made it better, and what you would either dial down or abandon altogether next time around. To move this idea on, do you stick with the same originating team or do you swap some of the team out for a while, to give them a break and a chance to review? Farmers used to let fields lie fallow in rotation, so that the soil recovered and was ready to give when the time came. Is this the case with some of your colleagues? Or do they need some renewal – the human equivalent of fertilizer – like training or a coach – to get them prepared for the next time? To get a great harvest you need to prepare the conditions. Sunlight is knowledge, the soil is the basis for the growth – that is, your team and their capabilities. It's a strange analogy, but taken to its extreme the harvest you have now can sustain your department through a time when things aren't so good.

While we're harvesting, we should celebrate what we've achieved, even as we use that time to learn and prepare for our next season. It's often forgotten that all the participants need a measure of recognition – it could be a note from the board, an extra day off, something on their personal record that recognizes they helped deliver a project. This is particularly relevant if your company has a tendency to recognize only the team leaders/managers who shepherded the project. The success was built on teamwork and the plaudits should be shared. Otherwise, you run the risk that your colleagues might not embrace the next project so enthusiastically.

Once you've harvested – namely got your new idea/project to market and launched it successfully – can you preserve some of it and use that to create your next iteration? Is there a next, deliverable step from what you have now? Can you use the seeds from this project again?

Or can you take the chaff – the elements without value – and use them as a resource? In recognizing the mistakes we made along the way and opening up about them, we stop the same mistakes being made again and again. We're all aware of the quote about doing the same thing repeatedly and expecting a different outcome, but this can be an easy trap to fall into. You can blame the timing, or a distraction or any other outside consideration – but considering the impact of events outside your control is a good tool for learning. If your product launch didn't happen because the regulations changed, do you need to join a trade body which might anticipate that? Or think about engaging with the authorities so you were aware it might happen? Do you know how vulnerable some of your key components are to the vagaries of weather, transportation or other issues? In the comfort of your harvest, consider what areas might prevent the next project being derailed. It is considerably easier to do this in the glow of a great idea that was brilliantly executed than sitting in the ashes of something that never worked out, so enjoy it. It is through this enjoyment that you'll get the insight and the power to move on and deliver the next great idea or proposal. Use this time to harvest and reap the benefits of all your hard work. You all deserve it.

Take Action

Discard the chaff, celebrate what you achieve, review the learnings (both good and bad) and keep the best seeds for the next project. Make this an exercise that you keep as part of the working rhythm of your team. Create a regular forum for shared learnings.

Listen hard

According to the personality profiling technique of communication dynamics, there are four main types of communicating at work, and most people fall into one of the main types.

Two of the four profiles are characterized by a propensity to tell others what to do: these are the Driver profile (focused on getting stuff done) and the Expressive profile (focused on people management).

The other two profiles are Analytical and Amiable. The former is about tasks, the latter about people. Both are characterized by the tendency to ask questions rather than to tell.

A good workplace has a mix of all four styles. Many workplaces that contain all four styles are also troubled by the tendency for the Drivers and Expressive communications people not to listen to the others. People who love to tell people what to do usually do not have much time or energy for good listening.

Sometimes listening hard is exactly what you need to do to come up with a creative solution to an ongoing problem.

Sally was running a team of people who were providing hard analytical data solutions to a large multinational client. Her team were bonused on a service level agreement based on a score out of 5. When it came to her first annual review, she was devastated to see that the score her team received was 2.3. She was also bemused. She had overseen the work, and believed it to be to a very high standard. She immediately asked for a face-to-face meeting to discuss the disappointing review, which was going to cost her team, and the company, significant income.

When she arrived for the meeting the managing director of the client firm welcomed her into the room and offered her some tea and cookies. He began by saying that the work overall had been very good: not only was the analytics revolutionary for his team, but they had already seen a positive upturn in business as a result of acting on the advice. He then said: 'You're probably wondering why the score was so low? To be very honest, your team make my team feel very uncomfortable. They are taking them to a level that makes them feel like they don't have the same agency and empowerment over their jobs, and this is significantly impacting the culture and happiness of my team.'

Sally was floored. She hadn't expected this. The fact that the quality of the work was appreciated meant so much, yet also so little because the score was discretionary and the managing director had prioritized his people's happiness. (He was probably an Amiable to Sally's Driver).

However, when she thought about this and the work across the year, she realized that she had missed the signals. When the work had won only a mediocre reception, she encouraged the team to double down and make it more detailed and radical. She had failed to interpret the signals; failed, in all honesty, to listen to what was really going on.

There's always a clue, and it is not necessarily what is said out loud. When Sally considered this, she recognized that the appropriate action across the period of the contract was not more hard work on the data, but more time spent listening to how the work was really being received and diagnosing how to sell it better so that the whole team was truly comfortable.

Steven R. Covey, author of *The 7 Habits of Highly Effective People*, believes that most of us fail to listen hard. We might ignore the other person because they aren't telling us what we want to hear, we might pretend to listen and utter a reassuring 'Hmm' every now and then. Sometimes we're selective and just hear what we want to hear. And even if we are paying attention, we still might not really grasp what is going on, especially if the person we are talking to says they are fine and OK. (In the bestselling *Three Pines* series of novels, Louise Penny coins the term 'F.I.N.E.' to mean 'Fucked up, Insecure, Neurotic and Egotistical', and therefore not fine at all.)

Covey instead describes the art of empathetic listening, going beyond what is said on the surface and allowing the real truth of the other person's perspective and emotions to emerge.

If you listen really hard, a creative idea will emerge. In Sally's case it was to change the way in which her team worked to ensure that they explained every step to the client and helped them come up with new ways of doing things instead of telling them what to do. Her next bonus score was 4.75 out of 5.

Take Action

Practise empathetic listening. Empty yourself of the need to be right. Be patient, and enter into the other person's frame of reference. Don't just fix things; make sure that you fix things collectively as a team. If you are by nature a fixer, write yourself a reminder in a notebook or on a laptop: *Stop fixing things, keep listening.*

Do things in the wrong order

Beginning, middle, end. That's the way it works, isn't it? All very logical and sequential and perfectly sensible. But quite reductive if you're trying to make change happen.

Think about starting at the end, perhaps. It gets you away from the initial faltering trip points, where you don't know where to begin. Perhaps deciding what the end would look like and feel like is a better operating point. We're familiar with a situation where the end user is actually taking more time to do something than before the 'improvement' because no one had considered how the executional element would be delivered. No one in the improvement team had thought to consult the end users; they just fell in love with an idea and did it. Before you ask, the 'improvement' now involves asking customers their unique customer ID, their memorable word and another identifying point. No one had thought it would be useful to tell the consumer they would need this information at the point of delivery, so the team members now often have to wait for customers to find all the information or do a long manual override of their own internal process. This leads to irritated customers, harassed team members and a longer transaction time. 'If only someone had asked us,' said a team member. The result would have been less harassed customers, and fewer front-line team members who find themselves the focus of anger and feeling that they are doing a bad job. Not so much of an improvement, then.

The other issue that can come from starting at the beginning is that you evaluate ideas as they are proposed. That sounds eminently sensible except that you're not comparing the ideas as a whole, and you're opening yourself up to the risk that how you run the meeting might suppress your best idea. For example, it's just before lunch, the meeting has gone on for three-plus hours and people are fidgety and hungry. A suggestion is made that seems at first glimpse to be the answer. It gets approval because everyone has sat through 15 or more other ideas and this is the chance to get out of the room and actually do their job. It would be far better to vote for the top three or top five and then come back to those rather than want to have a 'winner' that might be the result of boredom or the lure of a chicken and avocado sandwich. If doing that, get other people rather than the originator of the idea to work on the next stage of the process so that a less biased view comes into the analysis. You want the best ideas to go through, not the one Simon shouted about for so long that people caved in and agreed to just to stop him talking.

By starting in the middle, you can try to assume that you have got a winning idea or process and that you're planning how you implement it throughout the organization. History is littered with examples of armies who have swept all before them, only to fail because their supply lines are too stretched. By starting in the middle, you can fully analyze the capacity that your company and team have for change. If your busiest time of year is the fourth quarter, don't plan to have a new operational system that starts on 1 January. Yes, it has a feel-good sense of *New Year, New Start*, but trying to train busy teams, reboot the system and then start without hitch in the New Year is delusional.

They have probably been away from work over Christmas and can't remember their passwords, and the break has regularized the idea that afternoons are for watching films and eating chocolate. Get them back in, trained and refreshed, and then 1 February is deliverable. Those few weeks can make a big difference.

If you're starting at the end, make it about your customers. Ask yourself: *What do we want our customers to feel about us if this works? What three things would make our colleagues' jobs easier, more enjoyable or more fulfilling? What would success look like if we made a change?* Linear isn't always the answer – and it can even be your problem.

Take Action

Don't do things in the right order. Start at the end, or in the middle. It might just be the solution you need, and the wrong order of doing things might be right.

What would your worst enemy do?

Well, of course, you don't have enemies, which would imply that your company finds itself in a *Game of Thrones/Succession* situation. Good if you like dressing up in the first instance; not climate-friendly with all those private jets in the second.

Thinking like your business rival can be a very useful practice for creativity. You need to understand your enemy clearly and be capable of predicting what they would *actually* do rather than what you would do in their place. This piece of insight comes courtesy of a piece in the *McKinsey Quarterly* written by Courtney, Horne and Tan. As they point out, history has taught us that we live in interdependent times – your company's survival may depend on the prospects of your competitors in keeping the whole market viable. Their Merger and Acquisitions path is as important as yours.

By thinking about what they would do, you can explore new ideas within your market because they may have a different approach to product development or a slightly different market sector that they target. Above all, remember that they have teams that are not exactly the same make-up as yours. So, start by thinking about how your organizations differ in the way that they operate at both an organizational and an individual level. Think like your enemy and what their next best move should be and how they would deliver it. Is it an improvement to a current product or a brand-new idea? If they did that, what would your company do?

On a personal level – who makes those decisions and what are they driven by? What is influencing their decisions? Are they at a stage of their business where they are at the end of a long-term incentive scheme? If so, they might be less predisposed to do anything new or radical because it might affect their payout. Or are they new and keen to make their mark on the company? Once you know what is guiding their choices, you will find that this approach – becoming your own worst enemy – can deliver real competitive insights that can help you make better decisions. It's all too easy to make assumptions about what might happen next in any market, but an educated guess isn't what top management should be using in working out market development, those assumptions need backing up.

In the McKinsey piece, the authors discuss two different approaches taken in the fast-food industry to the same question. Faced with the realities of an obesity crisis and societal concerns, the market has responded with two very different approaches. McDonald's has altered its menu, now offering apple slices, carrots and other healthier options. At the time of writing, Burger King hadn't followed that path and was promoting high-calorie offerings with a campaign of cheeky and politically incorrect advertisements. As the larger player, McDonald's approach reflected its position as the lightning rod for concerns around obesity. As the smaller, challenger brand, Burger King saw the opportunity to cherry-pick a market segment among the less health-conscious consumers.

When you are playing the role of your worst enemy in your ideas generation, think about what they would do with your resources and people. They don't care about your *Oh but we mustn't change that, we've always done it that way* thinking. They don't care who they might upset or have to placate – they're the enemy, it's their job. You should be like them and think about what you can leverage, what you need to protect and what skills, people and acquisitions might change your company for the better. The upside of this role play is that now you know them so deeply, you can use that insight to make sure you get the best ideas and innovations first.

Take Action

Define the enemy to the business or the project. Why are they the challenge, and what can you do to pre-empt their next action, or outsmart their thinking?

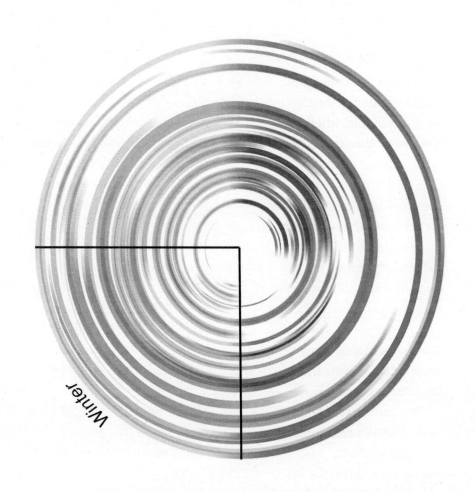

Winter

CHAPTER SIX

Winter – transformation

Sometimes the toughest problems to solve need a complete transformation of the creative approach. Such is the case when there are no green shoots, when the ground is hard, when darkness surrounds, and when optimism fails, when business is moribund and threatened by new competitors or new platforms.

In 2010 the internet entrepreneur Martha Lane-Fox was commissioned to write a report about the state of the UK government's digital framework. Her response was to condemn it as unfit for use. Among other criticisms, she pointed out that: 'Government publishes millions of pages on the Web, via hundreds of different websites. Most of these sites are still run as silos within departments. This fragmentation leads to significant duplication of functions and technology, and means the overall user experience is highly inconsistent.' Her conclusion was that a central body be created and put in charge of delivering a government website that was useful, streamlined and designed to serve the citizens of the UK.

The Government Digital Service (GDS) was created as a result, and its journey is a case study in radical creative reinvention.

In 2010 Martha said the government's websites were not fit for purpose. In 2016 the United Nations ranked GOV.UK, the single web domain for British government, the best in the world. Scores of government transactions became simplified and digital by default. As Francis Maude, head of the Cabinet Office at the time, wrote: 'People who wouldn't have dreamed of working in government signed up for the ride, proud to become public servants . . . cumulatively, our efficiency programme saved over £50 billion in five years.'

Andrew Greenaway, Ben Terrett, Mike Bracken and Tom Loosemore, the authors and leaders of GDS, gave an excellent account of this period. In *Digital Transformation at Scale: Why the strategy is delivery*, they set out principles for focusing on speed, agility and the right new technology to take a moribund situation and create real change.

Don't put new technology in a siloed department. It needs to be at the heart of what you do – and you must allow it to change everything that you do. Henry Ford once said, 'If I had asked people what they wanted they would have said faster horses', a frequently quoted observation and one that remains true today. Organizations that struggle with change are often wedded to the rhetoric of transformation rather than delivery.

Don't use slow data. It is crucial to be open about advances and setbacks and to do so quickly. Measure, then report in real time (not in retrospect) and change what you do as a result. Too many organizations and teams are sitting on lots of data and not doing anything positive with it other than massaging it to justify notional progress.

Don't follow the herd. When GDS was set up, mobile apps were on everyone's wish list and every minister wanted their own. Suppliers were queuing up with expensive build plans. GDS blocked most of them. The system was not ready for them; they just sounded like the latest thing to have. Too many leaders spend time talking about the company's embracing of the latest digital fad while at the same time their team's computers take 20 minutes to wake up each day, wasting cumulative hours of employees' time. That is the thing that you should fix before you adopt the latest trend.

Do have a mission. And make it practical and achievable by a specific date that is in line of sight (i.e. not in years but in months or weeks). GDS' ultimate aims included transforming government, improving public service and saving billions. The immediate goal was to set up the new cross-government website: GOV.UK. You need an attainable goal to build momentum.

Set out how you are going to work, make this transparent, available to everyone and applicable to the task. In the case of GDS, they had 10 design principles from the start:

Start with user needs. Do less. Design with data. Do the hard work to make it simple. Iterate, then iterate again. This is for everyone. Understand context. Build digital services, not websites. Be consistent, not uniform. Make things open, to make things better.

GDS was a disruptive creative force within government. As such it faced its own problems, even when the extent of its success became apparent. It regarded its mission as disruptive to the status quo. For this to succeed, a senior political figure as stakeholder was essential – this is where Francis Maude came in – to uphold the positive outcomes of this disruption in a culture where collaboration and indeed office politics are the norm. It also needed leaders who had experience of digital transformation in organizations that had themselves gone through radical change. Mike Bracken had led the digital revolution at the *Guardian* newspaper, Tom Loosemore had been responsible for the digital strategy at the BBC.

Above all else the right culture is crucial for creative transformation. The team had new ways of behaving from the start: stand-up meetings where presenters were heckled if they used acronyms; Post-it notes on walls to create plans for the week; a public 'Hello World' blog celebrating initiatives; an ability above all to be comfortable with working things out going along, winning arguments as they arise and not expecting to know all the answers from the beginning. The question asked was: *What can we do to make things better this week than last week?*, rather than trying to boil the ocean.

When change seems vast and unobtainable, chunk it up. Identify the barriers and ask: *How might we make this better?* Those three words: *How might we* can bring the first sliver of light to a dark landscape. Find some quick wins, make them visible by using metrics that reflect real progress (these might be different from the standard ones your business uses). Tell real stories about how what you're up to is creating change for the better. Don't underestimate the power of positive conflict and challenge. As the authors of change at GDS have said: Don't just break rules, invent new ones, because the chances are that lots of people are fed up with the old ones.

Here are 13 techniques for creativity when the darkness of winter feels like it has taken hold.

Uproot and destroy
Burn bridges
Go outside
Deliver long-term success
How can you get people to want much more?
Plan to get it up and running in six weeks
Spend a million
Be extravagant
Strip it back – make it smaller and simpler
Quick win
Push the idea until it scares you
Give the past a vote (but not a veto)
Hibernate

Uproot and destroy

Probably, on reading that subheading above, you've done a double take. *Hang on, we're spending all this time and technique on creativity and you're telling me to rip it all up? How can that make sense?* Perhaps, though, it has occurred to you that there are a number of horticultural references in this book, so you recognize that *uproot and destroy* does indeed have a place, not only in your garden but also in your approach to creativity.

Sometimes, in a garden there may be plants that are still flowering, holding their own against the snails and yet not thriving – they're a bit leggy, or not producing as many flowers as they once did. So, the best thing to do is uproot them and make way for something new. We're not suggesting that if Simon from Key Accounts is looking a little less than perfect he should be taken out of his role, but instead that you carefully examine some of your existing ways of working and make a decision – is it time to replace them? Or to put them in a different place where they might thrive? In Simon's case this might mean a new client patch or product to develop.

It's easy to let things carry on if there is just a gradual diminution of effectiveness or use – we convince ourselves that the situation is just temporary, or that it will revert to normal (whatever that means). So over time, we slide into a lesser version of our previous way of working, thinking that if it's been acceptable before, it should stand the test of time. However, there is no second flowering of an idea or a process once that idea or process has started to decay. Businesses can't continue if they only look to the past. So, what we're suggesting is that you uproot those ways of working and, if appropriate, take the new growth – ideas that are just coming on stream or which could still flourish – and give them a little more care and support. And those elements that aren't flourishing need taking out permanently. Colleagues who don't want to change are a frustration. We're sure you've all heard the phrase *But there was nothing wrong with the old system, why do we have to do things this way?* It's a hard task to have to drive change through when certain people just don't see why they should have to alter one iota of their working lives. It sounds boring to most of us, doesn't it? Yet some colleagues love that continuity. This is where you need to destroy. You cannot have parallel ways of working – one old, one new – existing side by side. It's like putting a fresh new plant next to one that has a problem; you run the risk of cross-contamination.

If there is a process that needs to go, you have to take it all out, including the roots. (Yes, that could involve being a bit hard with Mary, who doesn't like to change and is very good at her job. However, having an entire team unable to move forward because of Mary makes no sense.) You might – in fact, you will – feel a bit bad that you're becoming the enforcer of new ideas and operations. But you can't get to the next stage of where you need to be, by trying to accommodate everyone and everything that might entail. Of course, you will use logic and persuasion and charm to explain why you need to uproot and destroy. You'll make compelling arguments about the need for a fresh, new start without any remnants of the old ways hindering progress. Uprooting gives all your colleagues a fresh start, with new opportunities and the chance to grow. Why wouldn't you welcome that prospect and the excitement it could bring?

Take Action

You cannot have a thriving organization if you are afraid to take some radical action when it is needed. Sticking with the old ways because people are used to it, can mean that you destroy any chance of a thriving culture. If a tough decision needs to be made, then make it, follow through and give new ideas and ways of working a chance to deliver. Get the team together, ask them what they are doing that feels like a waste of time or which could be done in a better way, and then be ruthless about acting on this.

Burn bridges

Brian Eno, the musician, composer and producer, has worked on many albums released by iconic artists including U2, Talking Heads and Damon Albarn. Remember Roxy Music? Eno was the co-founder and synthesizer player on many of their hit songs. He's an innovator in ambient music, a genre some claim he invented with the album *Ambient 1: Music for Airports* released in 1978.

In 1975 he published Oblique Strategies. These were a set of cards to be used in the studio, or in any creative situation when you are stuck.

Subtitled: 'Over 100 worthwhile dilemmas' and authored by Eno and his friend Peter Schmidt, they are still for sale on Eno's website. The cards contain just a few words, and it is up to you to interpret them to fit your situation. They have inspired some of the techniques in this book, and we recommend that you take a look.

One of the techniques from Oblique Strategies is this one: burn bridges. At least, this is our interpretation of Eno's advice.

Stan Lee was the co-creator of Spider-Man, the X-Men, Thor, the Incredible Hulk, Iron Man, the Fantastic Four, the Avengers, Ant-Man and the Wasp, Nick Fury – and still more Marvel household names. He was born in 1922 and started work at 17 as an assistant at Timely Comics. The interesting point of his career came in the early 1960s, a time when most of the characters that are famous household names now, came into existence.

Until this point comics were highly disposable and aimed at seven-year-old boys; this was the standard and profitable business model.

Stan Lee spent years churning them out, and didn't really love them or believe in them. No one in the business wanted comics the way that Stan Lee wanted to write them, with flawed characters who were far from all-American perfect heroes. And nobody wanted comics drawn as the peerless artist Jack Kirby wanted to draw them (he had been fired from DC Comics for not sticking to their traditional vision).

Stan had had enough. He was on the point of quitting a job that was increasingly boring and mind numbing, and deep down he still thought he was going to write the Great American Novel (an ambition since childhood). (He certainly did write great human stories, just not in novel form.)

His wife said to him: 'If you're going to quit anyway, why don't you first do what you really want to do with the comics. What is the worst that can happen? They can only fire you, and you are on the point of quitting anyway.'

So Stan burned his bridges. He developed a comic series like no other. A comic series that broke all the rules of the existing genre and business model. The first creation with Kirby was the Fantastic Four. It wasn't aimed at seven-year-olds, it was aimed at anyone who had ever suffered, ever struggled, ever needed hope. Spider-Man soon followed, a character whose own selfish mistake (trying to exploit his powers for financial gain) led to his uncle's murder. He might have had superpowers, but he also had guilt, remorse and teenage impulses. He was not an all-American hero.

A personal favourite series from Marvel, *X-Men: The Dark Phoenix Saga*, is one of the best descriptions of teenage girl turmoil we have ever read. Again, the lead character was far from perfect. Characters were flawed, consequences were real and team members fought with each other before coming together to work against a common enemy.

Sometimes at work, you can become very pragmatic about your career. You may reach a point where it is easier to second-guess what the client wants from you rather than challenge the brief or push the boundaries of creativity. You only need to look at most of the advertising and comms surrounding us to see a sea of conformity. Too often, all the advertisers in one sector follow the same route to market (think of those TV ads showing cars driving down a mountain road or through a cityscape) and the only distinguishing feature is the logo at the end. Our role in agencies is to drive competitive advantage. If you follow the crowd, this is not what you get.

Take Action

Sometimes you should go with the flow. And sometimes (more often than most people do) you should burn your bridges and follow your heart. 'Excelsior!' – as Stan Lee himself was fond of saying. If you have a dream, what is stopping you? Who is stopping you? Review this, consider this and then push ahead, regardless.

Go outside

Going outside is a transition, a transformation – and a readily available solution when anyone is stuck for ideas. Going outside can be the start of a new adventure.

There is, of course, more than one way to go outside: you can go through a door, step outside of your social or work bubble, dive into the natural world, exit your comfort zone, experience a liminal space.

The most fondly remembered example of going through a doorway in many UK childhoods is in *Doctor Who*, when the Doctor steps outside the Tardis and a new adventure begins – preceded of course by the sound of the Tardis landing. (It's always a bit disappointing if they just end up in modern-day Britain, even if the Daleks are attacking. Such a let-down – and inexplicable until you reach the age of understanding that the production budget ran out.)

Going through a doorway can signify the start of a new way of looking at things for us all. Inside is control and organization. Outside there may be chaos, randomness. Inside is known, outside is unknown.

In the workplace we all need to step outside the office bubble. If you are working with the public, you will do well to be curious about other people's lives. The cliché of the ad agency bubble – and the accusation that creatives are producing work for other people like themselves, for an audience of Soho House members – exists for a reason. Often creative awards will showcase work that pleases peers more than it excites the public. But great work transcends this to speak to consumers' lives and understand what they genuinely care about.

You can't plan for that in a big-city office bubble. You have to dive into the lives of the prospective audience, get outside of the office, and go where they hang out, where they live, and immerse yourself in what they care about. A high street will tell you more about the buyers of many products than going to the office. The *Back to the office* evangelists need to take note that time spent in a café in a suburb or shopping centre might be more insightful and inspirational than filling in Post-it notes with Sharpies in a meeting room. Yes, teams need to cluster, but not necessarily in city centres. Go outside of your normal office space.

Get outside into some nature. Studies have proved the impact of green spaces on mental health. If you can take your challenges, or the problems that need creative solutions, outside and sit with them there, you should find the outside helps your thinking to flow.

Go outside your comfort zone. This doesn't have to be extreme or stressful. It's necessary for growth. Psychologists have a term for healthy development and growth. Lev Vygotsky's concept of the zone of proximal development (ZPD) is the difference between what a learner is capable of doing unsupported, and what they can do supported. In other words, you don't need to be ultra-brave, you don't need to skydive. But do reach out to colleagues and mentors for help in stretching into the mildly uncomfortable zone. Go beyond your immediate capabilities. The rewards are immense.

You will know your own boundaries. For some, it's challenging their conservatism, for others it may be changing jobs or partners, learning a new skill or hobby or making new friends.

Go outside the space you are in. The very act of going through a doorway or a portal, being in a liminal space, is renowned in storytelling as magical. It is a transitional moment, the gateway from one state to another. Richard Rohr, an American Franciscan monk and writer, describes this space as 'where we are betwixt and between the familiar and the completely unknown. There alone is our old world left behind, while we are not yet sure of the new existence. That's a good space where genuine newness can begin.'

Liminal spaces can be uncomfortable. But many people believe that you cannot begin afresh until you have separated from the old – in jobs, in relationships and in self-care. In the nothingness of liminal space, you can recreate a new version of yourself. Surely that's one of the greatest acts of creativity of all.

> ## Take Action
>
> What is your usual haunt? Where is your comfort zone? If you are stuck, take yourself and your team somewhere different, somewhere strange; take them outside.

Deliver long-term success

Shamanism is one of the oldest belief systems. Beliefs incorporate a strong sense of family, ancestry and animism, the idea that spirits exist in every natural object, making respect for the environment core.

'Mankind does not end its existence because sickness or some other accident kills its animal spirit down here on earth. We live on.' Nalungiaq, Netsilik woman

Clearly with this perspective comes responsibility to the spirits of your ancestors which still surround you, and a long-term perspective about your descendants and their environment, reaching aeons into the past and into the future.

Contrast this with the immediate and short-term results driving many careers. Does your boss set you objectives with key performance measures checked monthly or quarterly? Do you get a reward or bonus only for meeting or exceeding them in the next 12 months? Is the brief you're working on focused on immediate returns or does it have any objectives for the long term?

If you look at the annual reports of many big corporate businesses, you will find a recommitment to the long term. Some chief executives now consider not only the triple, the quadruple but even the *quintuple* bottom line as a priority. So not just profit (and stakeholder management), but also people, planet, ethics and equity (i.e. fairness for society at large).

Our last book, *Belonging*, is packed full of evidence that starting with people, ethics and equity will enable you to drive profits in the medium and long term. But, of course, it's not just about what your boss or business says. It's what motivates you to get out of bed each morning and bring your best self to work. Feeling like you belong is crucial. You must also consider your personal legacy.

Clayton Christensen, the bestselling academic, business consultant and creator of the theory of disruptive innovation, wrote:

'On the last day of class, I ask my students to turn theoretical lenses on themselves, to find cogent answers to three questions: First, how can I be sure that I'll be happy in my career? Second, how can I be sure that my relationships with my spouse and my family become an enduring source of happiness? Third, how can I be sure I'll stay out of jail? Though the last question sounds light-hearted, it's not. Two of the 32 people in my Rhodes scholar class spent time in jail. Jeff Skilling of Enron fame was a classmate of mine at HBS. These were good guys – but something in their lives sent them off in the wrong direction . . . . One of the theories that gives great insight on the first question – how to be sure we find happiness in our careers – is from Frederick Herzberg, who asserts that the powerful motivator in our lives isn't money; it's the opportunity to learn, grow in responsibilities, contribute to others, and be recognized for achievements.'

When faced with any challenge, and however short term the brief might appear, try to see the bigger, more long-term, more expansive picture so that you get to a truly creative and truly satisfying solution.

Take Action

Take a longer-term perspective. Ask: *How does this deliver* really *long-term success?* Think like a shaman, considering what legacy your work on the brand delivers for the wider world and for the next generations.

How can you get people to want much more?

There seems to be a belief in certain circles that only the senior tier of management are the ones looking ahead and striving for the next level of success, eager to lead the company or their part of the company on to bigger, better things. The remaining employees are sheep-like, awaiting the instruction of these demigods, who know best and can see the bright future ahead of us. This type of reductive thinking is a zero-sum game. For one thing, it puts an enormous pressure on managers to appear all knowing and sure of the path ahead. Actually, when you're holding down a senior role in today's ever-changing world, knowing anything beyond the next month can feel a challenge. Plus, it's lonely if you're the one who is meant to be capable of managing seismic change *and* delivering a summer party that everyone will enjoy and remember. Oh, and all while hitting your margins without exceeding your opex, or capex, and while writing charts for the board report.

All too often, companies treat employees (or 'staff' as they sometimes call them, with a level of Downton Abbey-like hierarchy) as an amorphous mass, oblivious to what's going on around them. In fact, they can be your best brand ambassadors, the touchpoints for glitches in your systems, and the drivers for change in ways that might not occur to people who aren't on the front line, day to day. The big question is: How do we get our teams to want much more?

Firstly, our way of communicating needs to be clear and inclusive. When one person says: 'This is an exciting opportunity', some people fear a cut in the headcount or a pointless reorganization, and tell themselves: 'This has got nothing to do with me.' When asking teams to be creative, set out the problem with clarity and say why it needs solving and what the benefits to them will be. It is a simple move to feel disassociated and detached from any new initiative if you don't see what it will do for you. Be prepared to go into a lot of detail as to why this is important and the role your team can play in this new iteration.

Speak their language, too. Most people don't talk about end users, they talk about customers or clients. Frame how this change will make their interactions with clients better – quicker, more competitive, easier to deliver. Make it about them, as well as the company. There is no better guarantee that you will crush any further participation in future than asking your team to go above and beyond their usual job role and then failing to acknowledge it in any way. We need to praise, in a meaningful way, all efforts to be creative in problem-solving. Everything has a start, and by giving regular feedback and praise for progress, you get a cohort that wants to do better and deliver. The added bonus of this approach is that it encourages wider participation from the whole organization. It's much more enjoyable to be part of a group that is trusted to find new ideas and given clarity on progress and thanks for their efforts, than feeling that all those projects are just a new way to imply you're not quite good enough to succeed. That the slightest slip goes down against your name, even if the decision not to proceed was part of a bigger review of processes. It takes a lot for some people to put themselves forward to be part of new ideas, so being respectful of their sensitivity isn't just good management, it's about being a good human being.

Giving your team confidence in that manner is a key part of building a creative powerhouse in your company. If your voice, no matter how tentative or shaky, is listened to and accommodated, you'll learn to feel that you're valued and that there is more that you can do. Of course, it won't always be perfect, but in working through ideas they can change and perhaps adapt to areas other than the problem at hand, you get two issues solved at the same time.

Take Action

If you focus on motivating and empowering your employees and colleagues, you will give them confidence to reach for the stars. Make sure that they all feel like their opinions are valued, and that their ideas are heard and actioned. If they want more for your organization this will be mirrored in the outside world.

Plan to get it up and running in six weeks

One of the issues that we've come across is when teams realize exactly how big the problem/opportunity is that they're being asked to address. *Let's change the way we do . . . everything. No boundaries, explore every angle, nothing is off limits.* A huge and possibly impenetrable task when there are 15 of you tasked with rethinking how an entire company works. Our innate desire to do things properly and leave no element subject to chance means that of course you'll want to look at everything. Which takes time and consideration. Before you know it, six months have gone by and all you're agreed on is that having Pancake Day in the canteen doesn't work because the demand is too high and the catering team hate the pressure it puts on them when they have to disappoint people. This is hardly market-leading thinking that will propel you to the next level of efficiency and relevance.

Why not impose a discipline that makes action the focus? This works in two ways: it gives the innovation team a specific time period, removing the worry that this specific project is going to absorb them for an unspecified period that may impact their regular role. It also means that those six weeks are a time focused on results, not peripheral factors.

For this to happen, you'll need to be ruthless in what your scope of work is. Exactly what is it that has to be achieved? Three improvements in process? A better end-user experience? This step will define who you get to work on your project, and also gives them a highly defined role. Experience has taught us all that everyone has an opinion on whether it should be a certain shade of blue for the new tote bags, or if we should have a view on wearing shorts in summertime, but people rarely feel so excited about hand dryers and their deployment in a new office. The fact is that the easy questions are sometimes addressed because the sheer scale of what we're asking is just too overwhelming.

Next, what steps have to be followed? Sequencing is really important and there is no point in rushing all out, only to find that you have missed a small but vital step. Your aim is to build a stable and viable output, not a house of cards.

The gritty element is defining who is responsible for each step – and the key element here is the *responsible* and *accountable* part. Your colleagues must own their own section and feel committed to it. It is worth remembering the role that psychology and team dynamics play in a fast-paced and dynamic situation. It's not going to work if allowances are made for colleagues who haven't quite got around to doing their bit. The need to build a sense of being an elite and capable team – the SAS or Navy Seals of the problem, all in it together – is key. If people can't manage the pace, replace them. As quickly as you can.

At the risk of sounding obvious, clarifying inputs and resources must be done before you start your six-week sprint. Get your meeting rooms booked, have enough laptops and any other equipment ready to go, and also consider having a core team with drop-in specialists. The specialists can play a key role in two ways. They bring a specific level of knowledge to part of the work and they also refresh your casting. If you are working very hard and feeling the pressure, another colleague turning up and expressing excitement and delight at what you've achieved is a real boost. Of course, this requires a managed selection in terms of those drop-ins, as no one wants to hear that everything they are working on will never happen in real life according to the office pessimist.

Take Action

Add a strict time constraint to the initiative. Go backwards – if it is to be completed in six weeks, what do we need to do in the first three days, the first week? Set unreasonable benchmarks and amaze yourself by what can be achieved by breaking things down and working fast.

Spend a million

Spend a million on your solution. Is that a huge amount? Depends on the context.

In 2023, buying a 30-second ad in the US Super Bowl cost $7 million. In 2020 the UK government spent over £160 million on advertising – mainly on safety announcements because of COVID.

Compared to this, one million won't get you very far. On the other hand, you can kick off an ad campaign on TikTok for $500, so in that context a million is lavish. It's all about context.

Exploring how far a million will take you can be a route to generating lots of different types of ideas. And it doesn't have to be a million dollars or pounds. A million Moroccan dirhams is more like £80,000 or $98,000. Perhaps that is more your project budget scope.

Or what about thinking about it in terms of time? Can you devote one million seconds – 11½ days – to the project across your team? Can you spend one million minutes – 694 days (or more than 2½ years given a five-day working week)? If you could, what would you do and how would this be different? And if you could raise £1 million, how would you do it, and what difference would it make?

In February 2021 Hollywood stars Ryan Reynolds and Rob McElhenney confirmed their acquisition of Wrexham football club, an impoverished team in North Wales. During the course of the next two years the team has had a rollercoaster ride, documented in the FX series *Welcome to Wrexham*. At the close of the 2023 football season Wrexham were promoted to the Football League, EFL League 2, for the first time since 2008.

The acquisition is a great piece of storytelling, and the sincerity of the new owners is currently not in question. The amount the pair spent on transfers, buying in new players, in the first season: just over £1 million. For Wrexham that cash made all the difference. An injection of £1 million, and the publicity that the owners created, has changed the fortunes not only of the club but of the town.

If one million is a relatively small amount in context, try thinking about a minimum viable product (MVP). This is a solution that was created by software developers to reduce the outlay for big projects. It's a product with just enough features to interest users, and provide early sales and feedback for development. The idea is to create the new product quickly, get feedback and then reissue. Jeff Bezos, one of the world's most successful entrepreneurs, kicked off the online shopping revolution with an MVP. He began selling books online, and originally, when a customer ordered a book, he'd buy it at a store and ship it to them. From this humble MVP came the empire that is Amazon today.

If a million seems a relatively large budget, either financially or in time (which it certainly is in many instances), then spending a million can inspire you to think about what time and money are worth. Think of it as a shorthand for a serious investment.

What can you create if you put all your resources behind this project? And what can you invest in to reap rewards in the long term? And equally, rather than buying good will with any budget, what will deliver the best return on investment (ROI)? If investing £1 million means making £10 million in the long term, then the context changes again.

In fact, for KFC Australia, investing $1 million in their Michelin Impossible campaign to win a Michelin star in 2019 for an outback fast food restaurant, produced an ROI of $91 million. The campaign enlisted the franchisee of the Alice Springs KFC, Sam Edelman, to try to get one of the most prestigious culinary accolades in the world. The campaign really resonated in Australia, with a chippy and challenger spirit, garnering huge publicity and, of course, reminding everyone who loved a KFC to go and get one. Of course, there was no star awarded, but the promotion earned national and international exposure, shifted people's perceptions of the restaurant chain, gave everyone a good laugh – and sold a lot of fried chicken.

> ## Take Action
>
> What does it mean for you to spend a million? Is this extravagant or miserly in context? Can you devote real time to the issue if not huge budgets? If you could invest a million, what would your return on investment (ROI) be?

Be extravagant

It's winter. Emotionally, if not seasonally. It's cold, everyone's bones are chilled. Now is the time for extravagance.

Think of children's parties where everyone goes home with a goodie bag. Think of how extravagant it can feel when a hotel room provides slippers. An extravagant gesture need not cost much. But the goodwill it generates will have a huge ROI. And the ideas that seem extravagant can be the ones that make a real difference.

Extravagance means extreme gestures. It means going beyond what is reasonable, perhaps as far as to the ends of the earth. Extravagant ideas are those that most people would shy away from and even mock.

We like to think of that scene in *Beverly Hills Cop II* where the protagonist Axel Foley cons Sidney Berstein into leaving him alone in his office. Foley produces 25 unpaid parking tickets and threatens to arrest Berstein. In response Berstein asks: 'Is there something that could make you forget about those tickets . . . like you'd be holding something in this hand and this hand you'd be concentrating on and the other hand [the one with the tickets] you forget about, you'd go: "What have I even got there?"'

What do you want from others, what extravagant gesture could you deliver that would mean that they'd forget about any barriers to giving you what you want? What could you put in their hand?

This might be extreme gestures of helpfulness to the people who you are managing or hosting. For example, the notion of *servant leadership* means that you always make sure that people in your team leave work on time or even early, have frequent breaks during the day, and really switch off when they were not at work. Too many team leaders take everything they can from their teams and consider themselves the boss, not the servant who is there to make sure that the team operates happily and without stress. The notion of the servant leader can be difficult to people who like hierarchy and who have fought their own way to the top. When you have had to deal with difficult bosses yourself, it takes a big soul to turn around and then, with extreme generosity, run a team as if you served them. But, of course, it pays dividends in terms of loyalty and dedication.

If you are selling a product, consider how generous you can be versus the competition. For instance, when Unilever launched Persil washing-up liquid in the UK, Procter & Gamble gave away Fairy washing-up liquid in supermarkets – three bottles for the price of one. This apparent extravagance not only ensured that shoppers didn't abandon the market leader for the challenger brand, but also took them out of the market for months and months because three bottles of Fairy lasts for ages.

In one big corporation the managing director took away the free biscuits at the tea point during the 2008 recession. This was meant to demonstrate due care for company budgets at a time when everyone was cutting back. The damage to morale was significant, though: a measure meant to reduce anxiety actually created worries for the stability of the organization. Another board member took it upon herself to reverse this ruling. Not only did the biscuits come back, but they conducted an all-staff survey to ascertain people's favourite biscuits. As a result the previous dull selection was replaced by the top three winners, including the very extravagantly chocolatey Orange Club (advertising strapline from the 1980s: *If you like a lot of chocolate on your biscuit, join our Club*).

Speaking of chocolate, the 2017 campaign for Snickers in Australia used an extravagant gesture to promote the brand. The long-standing strapline for the brand is *You're not you when you're hungry*, and the brand leveraged the concept of *hangry* – hungry and angry, which frequently coincide of course. The team created the *Hungerithm*, a hunger-algorithm which monitored social media posts and lowered the price of Snickers in 7-Eleven convenience stores as the internet got angrier. Prices dropped extravagantly as the social posts got angrier (hangrier), down to 82 per cent off the normal price. Sales grew extravagantly too.

Take Action

What is the most extravagant gesture you could make at this point? Don't just be generous, be extreme. This might mean extreme kindness, or extreme discounts. Take the norm and double down on delivering an outrageous version.

Strip it back

Rick Rubin is a legendary American music producer, co-founder with Russell Simmons of Def Jam, home to Beastie Boys, LL Cool J, Public Enemy and Run-DMC. According to MTV in 2007, he was the most important producer of the previous two decades. He's also produced Red Hot Chili Peppers, working on their breakthrough album, and his work with Johnny Cash brought the singer to a new audience. Jay-Z's '99 Problems'? Resolved by Rubin.

Radio host Lauren Laverne interviewed him and noted that most pictures of him at work show him not at a mixing deck, but lying on a sofa with his shoes off, or meditating.

He replied by explaining that he has no technical skill at all. His technique revolves around listening, understanding what is going on in his body while he listens, and looking for the times when he feels something: laughter, joy, the instinct to lean forward. He then strips back the musical performance to reveal more of that aspect.

His first music credit therefore – on LL Cool J's debut album, *Radio* – was not as producer but as *reducer*. He doesn't follow the rules of recording technique. He looks for the essence, the truth, the rawness of emotion, and takes out the clutter that stops that shining through.

Listening and feeling don't always feel like legitimate work. Here's the lead singer of Slipknot, Corey Taylor, explaining his view of Rubin's techniques, from an interview published in *The Ringer*:

> 'Let me give you the fucking truth of it. Rick Rubin showed up for 45 minutes a week. Yeah. Rick Rubin would then, during that 45 minutes, lay on a couch, have a mic brought in next to his face so he wouldn't have to fucking move. I swear to God. And then he would be, like, "Play it for me." The engineer would play it. And he had shades on the whole time. Never mind the fact that there is no sun in the room. It's all dark. You just look like an asshole at that point. And he would just stroke his huge beard and try and get as much food out of it as he could. And he would go, "Play it again." And then he'd be, like, "Stop! Do that over."'

This is a creative technique that lifts *good* to *great*. When we make arguments to persuade and to sell our work, we often rely predominantly on evidence and logic. Frequently we follow the rules of the category because to do so gives us credibility.

It takes bravery to know the rules, be expert in the category and then to follow a totally different path. It takes courage to strip back work to the essence. Individuals often add arguments and proof points to give them confidence in the presentation and selling of work. Adding logic, adding elements and feeling good with the list of evidence can give you comfort.

Listening, feeling, doing less and then stripping things back to their essence: that can give you greatness.

Take Action

Do less: look at the task list and strip it back. Instead of adding to the initiative, reduce it. Don't look for evidence, listen to how you feel.

Quick win

If you're in a group that requires creativity, it's probably there to induce (and produce) big changes. You'll be a multidisciplined and variously layered team and your task is clear. If it isn't clear, then you need to get clarity fast. Otherwise, you're not going to get anywhere meaningful, no matter how long you're given to achieve this aim.

We've stated elsewhere that confidence is infectious, and it's clear that momentum is too. All too frequently, you start off with a clear aim and a set of colleagues to help to deliver it, but you get nowhere and take a long time getting nowhere. You lose interest, the team loses momentum and vibrancy, and in the end you risk fading into that weird meeting you have to go to that's still in your diary 18 months after you initially started going, but you have nothing to show for it. No trial timeline, no customer feedback, no colleague feedback, just a blank. Attendance becomes sporadic and you find yourselves just drifting. Sound familiar?

So, what we need to have in place is a plan for a quick win. *Quick* obviously depends on the breadth of the project, but you can be the arbiters of what *quick* looks like in your case. If it's a new way of handling expenses, have a pilot group up and running in three or six months. Show progress and spread the word, and you'll get further. Clearly, you need a full perspective of the complexity and reach of your task, but if you agree that any progress or even signposting towards progress will happen in weeks or months, you're framing expectations. Expectations that exist both within your working team or the other stakeholders around it.

Important elements of quick wins are that they shouldn't involve any substantial capital expenditure. Anyone who has ever worked in an organization knows that suddenly asking for cash which isn't in the budget causes a headache. You then have to write a case for the spend and it goes through the relevant processes . . . which is painful, usually. You also have to decide and start work on your quick win as soon as you can. That sounds obvious, but waiting for all your elements to be in place could just be the brake on proceeding that you didn't need. Agree the win quickly, know your time frame and mobilize around it. If necessary, have a small subgroup who deliver the quick win. Be stringent in how you create that team, especially in terms of the skills and attitudes within it. You want a mix of strategists and deliverers. (Not that we're saying strategists can't deliver; it's more about spreading the task evenly. And some strategists are so in love with the strategy that they don't like what happens when reality strikes.)

Whenever organizations talk about change, people always think about how it's going to affect them – and that's entirely understandable and a very human response. When your team delivers a quick win, the idea of change and any notion that it's going to be difficult, or will affect team members adversely is in the process of being addressed. If the new expenses system means I don't have to carry around or store receipts for 3 months and then fill in an Excel sheet with 45 different cost centre attributions, then count me in! Oh, and when you say don't do your expenses every quarter, please forgive me for not relishing 45 cost centres cluttering up my brain every 4 weeks instead. If you make something too hard, the likelihood is that people will not give it their full attention. Which means the system doesn't work and someone in finance has to explain the process again. And again.

It's in that vein that the quick win works. You are breaking down a concept that can feel alienating and worrying into a process that is more human and understandable. So many times we, as organizations, make statements and express intentions that we feel are clear and inclusive. The problem is we're too close, and for those coming to them fresh, they don't read that way. Your quick win isn't just a win – it's a motivation, a reassurance and a first step to success.

Take Action

With a small team, work out what is your quickest win. Big changes are sometimes best achieved by very small wins that are amplified. Find the win, then promote it like crazy, and soon everyone will want a share of success, because everyone loves to win.

Push the idea until it scares you

'My creative partner and I when we were working together at an ad agency, we were together for nine years and they called us the cockroaches. And the reason they called us the cockroaches is because you have five teams working on a project and the client kills it all. The account lead asks for the next round of ideas. Client kills it all next round. And again.

You know what? All the teams start fading away, but my partner and I kept going.

And you know what? You know, many times we go, "Thank God the client did push us. We actually got to finally an award-winning idea." Most people go, "It's just too painful. I'm done. Let's move on. Move on to something else now."

It feels like a brick wall and it actually causes you to believe that you've reached the end. It's not the end and you have to understand that it's not the end.'

This is Benjamin Vendramin on creating ideas for ad campaigns. Vendramin is Chief Creative and Content Officer at agency EssenceMediacom in New York. He's won multiple Cannes Lions, the ultimate accolade for creativity in advertising. And he's convinced that great ideas are rare, and that even then, ideas are easy compared to the pain of delivering them. He adds: 'There are very few breakthrough ideas, ideas that scare you. Most are vanilla. And there's a reason that the world's preferred ice cream is vanilla. Everyone can agree on it. But ideas that no one's heard before, they are the ones that scare you. But if the idea doesn't make me a little nervous, a little scared, I don't think it's a great idea.'

Vendramin developed an idea for MGM Resorts which won the team a nearly impossible five Lions at the Cannes Festival of Creativity in 2018. Shortly after gay marriage was legalized in 2015 in the United States, the team realized that there weren't many same-sex love songs. They persuaded six iconic artists to recreate love songs with new lyrics, suitable for same-sex marriage celebrations, and released the album *Universal Love*, which included recordings from Bob Dylan (who rerecorded the classic '*She's* Funny That Way' as '*He's* Funny That Way'), Kesha, St. Vincent, Ben Gibbard of Death Cab for Cutie, Kele Okereke of Bloc Party, and Valerie June. Musical duo She & Him released their first original music in five years for the album, with two versions of the same song: 'She Gives Her Love To Me' and 'He Gives His Love To Me' so that people could choose the perspective that suited them.

Vendramin says the idea took a while to come to fruition, and it was crucial to find the right partners. It took the team time to find the right idea, on the right side of controversy, and it was important to reject anything that felt too safe. To deliver the idea took more resilience, and Vendramin says that if the whole team had not been passionate about it, had not believed in it, it would never have come to fruition.

If you find an answer, try pushing it further. Look at your ideas, scale them on a scale of 1 to 10 in terms of bravery. Then push the idea to 11. Or 15.

To empower courage in the workplace, it is fundamental to encourage psychological safety. If people feel scared to contribute, you're not going to get through to edgy ideas. You have to create an environment which is genuinely uninhibited in terms of creativity. Make sure the whole team feels that they belong, that they are listened to, and that they are valued. Consensus in the workplace can be a fine thing, but if it is reached too quickly, or if there is no tolerance for positive dissent and challenge, then it will not get you to a place of true creative edge and advantage.

Take Action

Don't accept the first set of ideas, or the second or the third. Keep pushing until you get to an idea that scares you. Make sure the team feel that they all belong, and that they belong to a team that pushes ideas to the edge.

Give the past a vote (but not a veto)

The world has changed, but the way that we operate in many spheres has not changed enough. This is true of many sectors. Not enough change.

It's true that this is one of the barriers to inclusion, equity and belonging. Newer tech has been shown to carry the prejudice of the past when algorithms endorse the biases of old. As algorithms invisibly permeate our world, constant vigilance is crucial. Our children need to learn to be as aware of this as they grow up in a world where their preferences are always reinforced, and potentially manipulated. We need to teach our children well in this respect.

Not enough change. There's a catch-22 which may be familiar to many when innovation is requested along with the requirement that it is proven to work from past experience. An impossible conundrum.

Crucially we are in danger of continuing to follow the rules of thumb or heuristics of the past in a world we know has changed irrevocably. In sector after sector, businesses follow the paths of the past. Stef Calcraft, the advertising legend, has heralded a new era of creativity: 'The world has changed, and the people we need to connect with have changed too. Our job is to understand what matters to them most, what they really care about, and give them more of what they want and more of what they need. If we can do this, we'll be more successful than ever before.' Yet so much thinking is stuck in old-paradigm, pre-internet thinking. We must transform how we work and how we create to build platforms and ideas that truly make a difference in today's transformed world. Back to Stef: 'We have entered a new creative era where the ideas we create can be more purposeful, more powerful, and inherently more active than ever before. We are all privileged to have this opportunity.'

This doesn't mean going back to previous ways of working reminiscent of the Mad Men era. This is the creation of a new way of working which harnesses the brand truth, the consumer reality and cultural relevance. It's hard to change. It's hard to throw off the shackles of the past. Yet this we must now do.

Find new ways to organize your teams and to incentivize creativity. A 48-hour workshop, with cross-discipline teams, incorporating clients, customers and outside agencies, where mixed teams compete for ideas, can accelerate change and foster lasting relationships. Change the brief, just for this workshop, and see what it fosters. If you are normally focused on growth, see what happens if the brief is about making a better society instead. If you are normally focused on efficiency, set a challenge about growth. This might seem as though it will sacrifice your current knowledge and experience, but it is only by killing old ways that the new can thrive.

Mordecai Kaplan, one of the great Jewish thinkers and a man who played a huge role in adapting religious practices for the modern era, said this: 'The past has a vote, but not a veto.' We need to pay respect to the past but not let it limit how we work today.

It's great to have perspective on past success, and it's important to incorporate the lessons of experience, but it is more crucial to be open to new ways of working to drive success in this complex world. Think of this as a golden age for creativity.

Take Action

You need to change how you work if you want to change the output. If you want to be more creative, reorganize the ways of working. Collaboration and cross-discipline teams that have a specific, time-limited goal, and which share the incentives to deliver, will lead you to different and more creative outcomes. Muscle memory is very sticky, and can slow change. There might be people in your stakeholder group who are wedded to the way they have always done things. If this is the case, listen to them, but don't regard their point of view as unarguable. It isn't change that is the threat, but not changing.

Hibernate

'Onwards!' or 'Forward!' is the very potent cry that seems to be prevalent at the moment. It's very reminiscent of *The Wolf of Wall Street* and its crazed, turbo-charged sense that as long as you were winning, going full pelt for the goal, you were a Master of the Universe. Even if you didn't really know where you were headed, just the idea of the committed full throttle was enough. It is no surprise that a large number of people found that approach rather wearing and not for them and decided they didn't want to be part of it. And thereby weakened the whole system, making it full of people in violent agreement who never listened to anyone else: they didn't have to, they were Masters of the Universe.

In contrast to this, there is a recognition that leaders with high EQ, who are empathetic with their teams, are much more suited to today's working practices. These types of leaders are probably happy with the idea of hibernating. We're not advocating that you sleep from late October until the warmth of spring awakens you, though those of us who find the party season at the end of the year a trial might welcome the notion. What we are talking about is recognizing that just stopping, even for a short time, can be a great idea.

Burnout is a real problem in today's workplace. Technology has meant that it's easy to be available for work from the moment you wake up until you go to bed (and your last action at night is to check your phone for any late emails). Nothing on the television that you want to watch? Opening up your laptop and clearing your inbox could be a great idea, don't you think? We've been told about someone who checked their emails while listening to a mindfulness app, on the basis that it addressed two things on their to-do list at the same time. Which rather negates the mindfulness, we think. However, the idea that you should be always on is so pervasive that it's hard to avoid. So our teams keep on and on, probably with diminishing returns, because they feel like they must. We know that the temptation to send a quick email at the weekend so it's off your to-do list is very tempting. The idea that you delay the delivery until Monday at 8 a.m. makes you feel that you're respecting boundaries. However, if you are a line manager who sends multiple messages over the weekend, so that at 8 a.m. your team experience waves of incoming random email, your urge to be efficient might be demoralizing for your team as well as being inefficient.

Hibernating is a good response to this. If you know that there is a defined deadline, you aim for it with purpose and intent. The structure that it creates can be a framework shaping how your team works. Then you hibernate, reflecting on what you've done and creating space to think. It's important to remember that motivation, like confidence, can be contagious. If you're in a team and you know the structure – that you're going to have some space – that's a great motivator. So, you're all moving in the same direction and you can keep each other going, if necessary.

Hibernation can be combined with a commitment to reflection and analysis, the necessary counterpoint to a full-throttle approach that always looks forward but never back and so might never learn from any mistakes or lessons that happened along the way. You need to be clear, though, that hibernation is not a time for eye-rolling or assigning blame – claiming, say, that Susanna and Manuel's failure to hit a deadline is the reason you're not where you want to be. This is a time for a calm and kind look back at what you have done, where you are on your pathway and what the best next steps are. It's also crucial to solicit the input of everyone involved to get a clarity of view. Don't just listen to the loudest voices; listen to all the inputs you have available. One of the most successful regenerations in sport took place under Sir Dave Brailsford, who turned a team of also-rans into multiple Olympic winners. He sought the views of everyone involved in the team – bike technicians, trainers, nutritionists and logistics colleagues, as well as the athletes – to create a team where incremental gains in each area all combined to create greater momentum. They took the time to hibernate – so why don't we?

Take Action

Slow things down, reflect, review, be calm, be kind. Regeneration might elude you unless you take time to stop, rest and recover for the coming of spring. Pause while you prioritize your physical and emotional well-being and that of the wider team. This will be a springboard for action, once you have all recovered your positivity and energy for change and creativity.

Guide to the Seasons

Here are some frequent business challenges to help you apply the creative techniques, because of course the calendar spring might be your business winter and vice versa.

I'm worried that we're falling behind our competitors
Customer feedback is mediocre
I can't make change stick
Look for the techniques in SPRING

We've been through lots of change, how do we get our rhythm back?
I'm worried about burnout
I'm bored and I want something new
Look for the techniques in SUMMER

My team isn't proud of what we do anymore, they are just dialling it in
Our business has had an extended growth period, how can I make sure it continues?
My team have worked together for a long time, how do we stay fresh?
Look for the techniques in AUTUMN

How do I navigate lean times?
We've just lost our biggest customer, what can we do?
A new start up is eating our lunch
Look for the techniques in WINTER

Afterword and Acknowledgements

Creativity is transformational, and we believe that it brings growth and hope to every organization.

Accountability and analytical skills are necessary, but they are table stakes. Creativity can bring the leap that drives innovation and also makes the workplace a more interesting and fun place to be.

We would like to acknowledge all the people we have worked with who have helped us to hone our creativity, and especially the ideas that Brian Eno and Peter Schmidt's Oblique Strategies have provoked, as well as the excellent Whatif? Techniques.

Huge thanks to everyone at Bloomsbury, with whom it is a pleasure and privilege to work especially Ian Hallsworth, Lizzy Ewer, Allie Collins, Caroline Curtis and Erin Brown. And, of course, thanks too to our magnificent and accidental agent, Clare Grist-Taylor, who makes us better at what we do.

As always, this book is dedicated to our families, without whom we would not be able to be our true selves.

Index

.